PRACTICAL PROJECTS FROM FINE WOODS

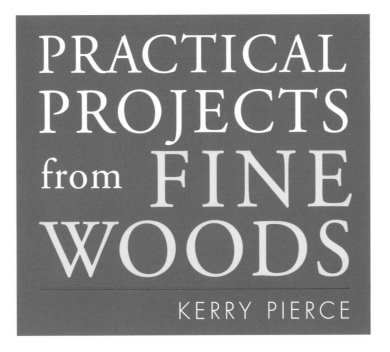

PRACTICAL PROJECTS from FINE WOODS

KERRY PIERCE

LARK BOOKS

A Division of Sterling Publishing Co., Inc.
New York

Published in 2001 by Lark Books, a division of Sterling Publishing, Co., Inc., 387 Park Avenue South, New York, N.Y. 10016

© 1996 by Kerry Pierce

First published in 1996 by Betterway Books, an imprint of F & W Publications, Cincinnati, Ohio

Editor: Adam Blake
Production Editor: Katie Carroll
Designer: Sandy Conopeotis Kent
Line illustrations: Kevin Pierce
Cover Photo: Pamela Montfort Braun
Some designs adapted from *The Book of Shaker Furniture*, by John Kassay (Amherst, MA: University of Massachusetts Press, 1980).

Library of Congress Cataloging-in-Publication Data

Pierce, Kerry.
    [Making elegant gifts from wood]
    Practical projects from fine woods / by Kerry Pierce.
        p. cm.
    Originally published: Making elegant gifts from wood. Cincinnati, OH : Betterway
Books, 1996.
        ISBN 1-57990-215-4 (pbk.)
        1. Furniture making. 2. Woodwork--Patterns. I. Title.

TT194.P53 2001
684'.08--dc21

                                                        00-049769

10 9 8 7 6 5 4 3 2 1

Distributed in Canada by Sterling Publishing,
c/o Canadian Manda Group, One Atlantic Ave., Suite 105
Toronto, Ontario, Canada M6K 3E7

Distributed in the U.K. by Guild of Master Craftsman Publications Ltd., Castle Place,
166 High Street, Lewes, East Sussex, England BN7 1XU
Tel: (+ 44) 1273 477374, Fax: (+ 44) 1273 478606, Email: pubs@thegmcgroup.com,
Web: www.gmcpublications.com

Distributed in Australia by Capricorn Link (Australia) Pty Ltd., P.O. Box 6651, Baulkham Hills,
Business Centre
NSW 2153, Australia

If you have questions or comments about this book, please contact:
Lark Books
50 College St.
Asheville, NC 28801
(828) 253-0467

Printed in Hong Kong

ISBN 1-57990-215-4

THANKS:

- Elaine, Emily, Andy, who walked around all this stuff for a month and didn't once threaten to move out
- Sal and Jim, who bailed me out when it looked as if I wouldn't get everything done in time
- Chuck (my brother, Kevin), who did the beautiful drawings on these pages
- Verne, who gave unfailingly good advice
- John McDonald, who let me try writing for money when no one else would
- Adam Blake and all the people at Betterway Books, who didn't fold up their tents and go home when I ran into problems

METRIC CONVERSION CHART

TO CONVERT	TO	MULTIPLY BY
Inches	Centimeters	2.54
Centimeters	Inches	0.4
Feet	Centimeters	30.5
Centimeters	Feet	0.03
Yards	Meters	0.9
Meters	Yards	1.1
Sq. Inches	Sq. Centimeters	6.45
Sq. Centimeters	Sq. Inches	0.16
Sq. Feet	Sq. Meters	0.09
Sq. Meters	Sq. Feet	10.8
Sq. Yards	Sq. Meters	0.8
Sq. Meters	Sq. Yards	1.2
Pounds	Kilograms	0.45
Kilograms	Pounds	2.2
Ounces	Grams	28.4
Grams	Ounces	0.04

Table of Contents

Introduction 9

Chess Table, 18

Shaker-Style Mirror, 30

Ten-Drawer Chest, 46

Shaker-Style Pedestal Stand, 62

Six-Drawer Chest, 86

Sheraton-Style Table, 102

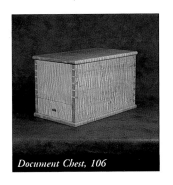
Document Chest, 106

Six-Wood Box, 118

ABOUT THIS BOOK

This isn't a book of original designs, although there are some here. It is, instead, a collection of pieces that a relatively experienced woodworker could build in a weekend or two or three. It is also a collection of designs that could help a relatively inexperienced woodworker acquire new skills and confidence.

Some of the designs are mine. Some are my dad's. A half-dozen are variations of Shaker originals drawn by John Kassay in *The Book of Shaker Furniture*, which is a wonderful source for any woodworker. Others are variations of a number of period forms.

INTRODUCTION

At the age of twenty, I took a job as yard foreman of a local lumber company. Although the title, foreman, sounded impressive, there was nothing impressive about the job. It was just hard physical labor for which I was paid little more than minimum wage. It did, however, offer access to good-quality construction-grade lumber at low prices. While I never cheated the company by, for example, putting #1 in the #3 bin so that I could buy it at the cheaper rate, I did profit from my position. If a truckload of #2 white pine arrived and if, while unloading it, I noticed a couple of boards that could have been graded #1, I set them aside and later bought them for my own use.

And I did use them.

Since my dad had been a carpenter and cabinetmaker throughout most of his adult life, I knew something about woodworking. I could tell a 2×4 from a 2×6. I knew what a casing nail looked like, and I could operate power equipment.

So at the end of my workdays in the lumberyard, after the overhead doors had been closed and locked, I used the company's table saws and radial arm saws and jointers to render that cheaply bought stock into properly dimensioned parts. Then I took them home and made things.

I didn't, however, make anything that I would now regard as furniture.

The pieces I built at that time, for the purpose of filling my apartment with useful objects—tables, shelves, cupboards—were all built of construction-grade lumber, all nailed together, and all prone to sudden and unpredictable collapse.

But at the time, I thought they were magnificent. After all, I'd made them. And they did work. I could put books on the shelves. I could lay papers on the desk. I could set a glass on the end table close at hand while I watched TV.

And, of course, my friends marveled at them.

But over a period of years, as I moved from apartment to apartment, taking with me these crudely made wooden objects, their shortcomings became increasingly clear. Nails simply won't hold furniture together. White pine is too easily dented and scratched. And 2×4s make inelegant table legs.

Several years later, married, needing furniture, I put together a toolkit consisting of garage-sale hand tools and a table saw. The hand tools were rusted and worn. The table saw was a handheld circular saw bolted to the underside of a stamped metal table, more a table saw in theory than in practice. Yes, there was a miter gauge and a round

blade with sharp teeth. But the saw was underpowered, with a rip fence that defied my best attempts at accurate alignment.

But the tools could be used, and with them I built another houseful of wooden goods. These were a bit more sophisticated than their predecessors. This time I used lap joints and glue. This time I turned screws into hardwood, rather than drive nails into pine. This time I used three coats of finish-from-a-can instead of the single coat that had protected earlier work.

Once again my friends obliged me by complimenting my work, but at about that time I'd begun to look at woodwork with a more critical eye. *Fine Woodworking* had recently made its appearance. Library shelves had become crowded with books on Shaker furniture and woodenware, Queen Anne reproductions and the magnificently executed furniture of eighteenth-century Philadelphia.

In spite of the kind words of friends, I'd begun to feel like an imposter. Clearly, the country was neck-deep in more knowledgeable, more talented woodworkers—my dad, for instance. While I was screwing birch fronts to plywood cases, he was building elaborate Chippendale reproductions with carving and turning and reeding.

So I studied. I bought more tools. I chose a home because of its shop space. I visited sawmills and bought my hardwood at the source.

Later, I began to sell my woodwork.

Later still, I began to write for woodworking magazines.

I became an expert?

Not at all.

The more I worked, the more certain I became of the inadequacy of my skills, knowledge, instincts. There was always more to learn. There was always somebody better.

And I think that's the way it is with woodworkers.

While in the shop, we may experience moments of accomplishment and satisfaction as we step back to admire a nearly completed piece, but later we recognize shortcomings, imperfections, errors. Later we see all the things that we might have done better if we'd only taken the time.

I think this is true for all of us, regardless of individual skill level. We work at this craft because we want to experience those moments of satisfaction when a piece begins to come together, but we recognize that, ultimately, the woodworking process is not so much an individual creative act in which an individual piece of furniture or woodenware is built; it is, instead, a lifelong pursuit of perfection.

—*Kerry Pierce*

1

CANDLEBOX

Cherry

Today, the beveled faces of raised panels are formed on the table saw or the shaper. These methods produce very predictable results, but the machines are noisy and dirty and leave surfaces that often require a fair amount of cleanup with a scraper and sandpaper.

The raised panels which form the lid and bottom of this candlebox were created with hand planes. This method is not only quieter and cleaner (and more historically accurate), it also produces a smooth, sheared surface requiring little attention with sandpaper.

MAKING THE CANDLEBOX

This simple but attractive candlebox is distinguished by its sliding top. The lid has beveled edges tapering so they can slide in grooves cut into the inside faces of the box's sides and one end. A carved, inset pull adds a decorative touch as well as providing a means for easy sliding of the lid.

After the lumber is milled to the required thicknesses, widths and lengths, cut grooves to receive the top and bottom panels. Next, cut the through dovetails at each corner (this procedure is discussed in chapter twenty-five). Bevel the top and bottom panels and assemble the case around the bottom panel, which is left unglued so that it can expand and contract across its width in response to seasonal changes in humidity. Complete construction by fitting plugs into the openings left at each corner at the ends of the grooves.

The open top of the candlebox lid reveals the grooves the lid rides in.

HAND-PLANING THE BEVELS FOR THE CANDLEBOX LID

1 First, make layout lines to mark the limits of the bevel. Make one line around the edges of the lid ⅜" from the lid's bottom surface. Make a second line on the lid's top 1¼" from the outside edges. The bevel will connect these two lines.

2 Plane the bevel across the end grain first so that any tearout occurring at the end of the plane's stroke will be removed when the adjacent bevel is formed. Although a jack plane can be used to make this bevel, it may be necessary to finish with a block plane which, with its lower cutting angle, produces a cleaner surface across end grain.

SHAPING THE PULL

1 With a marking gauge or a sharp knife, make a line parallel to and 1" from the unbeveled end of the lid. Position the stationary leg of a compass on that line halfway across the width of the lid. Draw an arc with the compass's pencil point.

2 Placing the tip of a flat chisel in the scored line, cut along that line, angling toward the arc. Using a wide-sweep gouge, make cuts from the arc back toward the scored line. Carefully lever up chips.

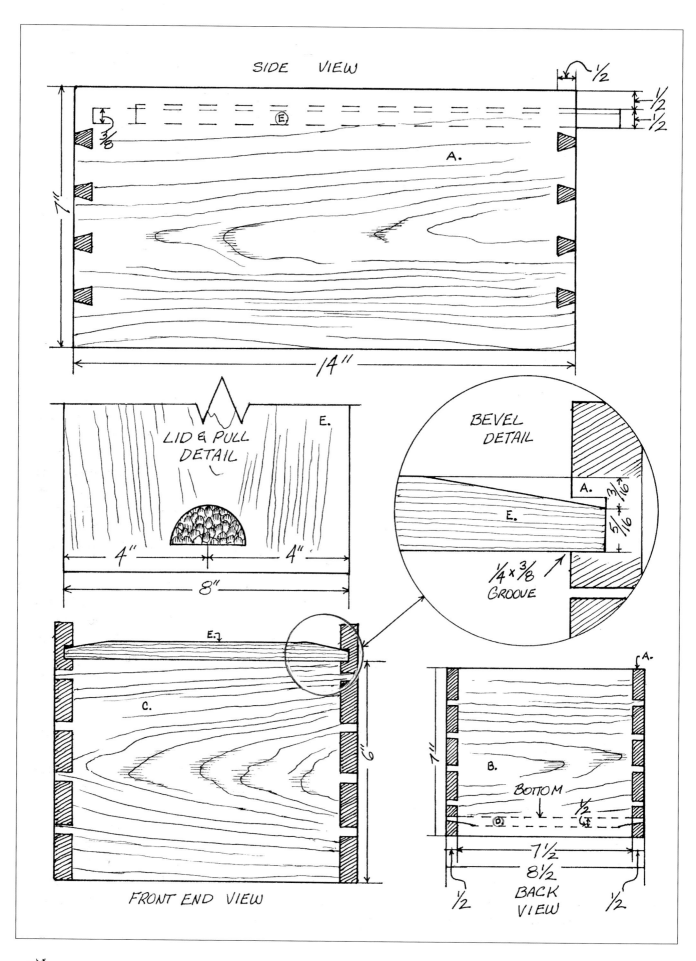

SIDE VIEW

½

½
½
½

⅜

7"

A.

14"

LID & PULL
DETAIL

E.

4"   4"

8"

BEVEL
DETAIL

A.
E.
3/16
5/16

¼ × ⅜
GROOVE

E.

C.

6"

FRONT END VIEW

A.

7"

B.

BOTTOM
½
G

7½

8½

BACK
VIEW

½   ½

SHAPING THE PULL (CONTINUED)

MATERIALS LIST			
A	Side	2 pcs.	½ × 7 × 14
B	End	1 pc.	½ × 7 × 8½
C	End	1 pc.	½ × 6 × 8½
D	Bottom	1 pc.	½ × 8 × 13½
E	Top	1 pc.	½ × 8 × 13¾
F	Plug	6 pcs.	¼ × ⅜ × ¼, shaved to fit

These are net measurements. Surplus should be added to dovetailed parts to allow them to be sanded flush.

3 Once the depression has been formed, you can give the pull a smooth surface, or, as I've done here, you can give it a bit of texture.

SAM MALOOF'S TWO-STAGE FINISH

Fifteen years ago, *Fine Woodworking* (issue no. 25) ran a profile of Sam Maloof, the California woodworker best known for his magnificent rocking chairs. Included in the article was a sidebar in which Maloof discussed several technical issues, closing with the recipe for his finishing mix.

My dad—who designed and built several of the pieces displayed in this book, including the crotch-grained chess table—began experimenting with Maloof's finish and found it wonderfully adapted to the small shop. After years of spraying lacquer, a toxic experience inevitably preceded by the emotionally toxic experience of attempting to vacuum every particle of dust from every shop surface, he found in Maloof's formula a finish that not only produced a very appealing surface but also, just as importantly, was impervious to dust contamination.

Preparation is no different for this finish than it would be for any other. Scrape the wood, then sand it with a variety of grits, finishing with a thorough sanding using paper no coarser than 220-grit. Then wipe the wood clean with a tack rag.

Maloof's recipe calls for equal parts mineral spirits, boiled linseed oil, and polyurethane varnish (an extra dollop of varnish seems to add body to the dried film).

Brush on this mixture liberally with only minimal concern for drips and runs—coverage is the focus at this stage. Allow the finish to set until it gets a bit tacky. Depending on temperature and relative humidity, this could be anywhere from ten to sixty minutes.

Wipe the surface with clean rags to remove any excess that has failed to penetrate into the wood.

As the finish dries, it lifts wood fibers and hardens them producing a rough texture. (This first coat acts as a sanding sealer.) Again, depending on temperature and relative humidity, this could take anywhere from one to three days. In humid Ohio, I've found it best to wait three days before sanding that first coat. Otherwise, areas of raised, roughened grain may not make their appearance until after the last coat has dried.

I use 320-grit wet/dry paper soaked in mineral spirits to cut away the raised grain. The thinner clots the removed material into a slurry which may help to smooth the surface; however, my reason for dunking the paper in mineral spirits is to unload the grit in order to get more mileage out of each piece of sandpaper.

Once you have sanded and thoroughly cleaned the surface with a tack rag, apply a second coat of the three-part mixture. It is particularly important that this coat (and any subsequent coats) be wiped clean. Any residue remaining on the surface will dry there and leave a roughened area.

Sam Maloof tops this finish with a layer or two of boiled linseed oil into which he's mixed enough shaved beeswax to achieve the consistency of cream. He applies the wax, allows it to dry, then buffs it out. You can achieve similar effects with a number of commercially prepared waxes.

2

BENTWOOD BOXES WITH TURNED AND CARVED LIDS

Walnut, Curly Maple, Cherry

Typically, bentwood boxes are fit with lids and bottoms cut on the band saw, then rabbeted either by hand or with a router. The boxes discussed in this chapter are a little different having lathe-turned lids and bottoms. This simplifies the process of cutting rabbets as they can be created very easily on the lathe. The use of the lathe in shaping lids and bottoms also opens up some intriguing design possibilities.

MAKING THE BENTWOOD BOXES

First, make a bending form for the main body of the box. This can be fabricated from any scrap that can be glued together to make up a sufficient thickness. This is then band sawn and sanded to the inside profile of the finished box. Undercut the face of the bending form at one point to allow for the thickness of the lapped material underneath the box's glue joint. Screw a thin strip of metal (I used a scrap of aluminum siding) to the form underneath which an end of the sidewall material should be inserted prior to being wrapped around the form.

At this time, saw a clamping caul (see photos, below) with a slightly greater radius than the bending form from scrap material. This caul will protect the sidewall material from the clamps.

The next consideration is the sidewall material itself. There are three possibilities. First, the stock can be resawn, planed and sanded to a thickness of ¹⁄₁₆″. Second, Constantine's Hardware sells ¹⁄₁₆″ veneer in cherry, walnut and mahogany, even though those thicknesses aren't listed in their most recent catalogs. Third, the sidewall material can be glued-up from two thicknesses of ¹⁄₃₂″ veneer, which is widely available in a variety of species. I would recommend using one of the new waterproof glues between the laminations, although I have built boxes using regular aliphatic resin glue to bond the thicknesses of veneer.

Then, soak the sidewall stock in a tub of cool water for twenty-four hours; dunk it briefly in warm water and take it directly to the bending form. Tuck one end of this softened, plasticized material under the metal strip on the bending form. Wrap the remaining length around the form and secure in place with clamps and the caul.

Four or five days later, remove the sidewall material from the form and cut the profile of the lap joint. A bench extension to which is nailed a piece of scrap sawn to the inside radius of the box simplifies the cutting of the joint.

Then, glue the lap, wrap the sidewall material around the form once again and clamp with the aid of the caul. This time, however, do not insert the end of the sidewall material under the form's metal strip. After being turned, attached the box's bottom to the sidewalls with four ¹⁄₈″ wooden pegs driven into predrilled holes.

CUTTING THE LAP JOINTS

1 This is the bench extension used to maintain the curved form of the sidewall material during the cutting of the lap. The clamping caul is visible on the right.

2 A lap joint is being cut on the bench extension.

3 Here, the glued lap joint is being clamped with the aid of the caul. Notice that the end of the sidewall material is not positioned under the metal strip as it was during its initial clamping for shape.

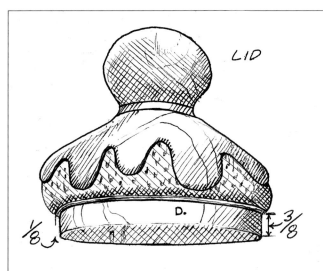

LID

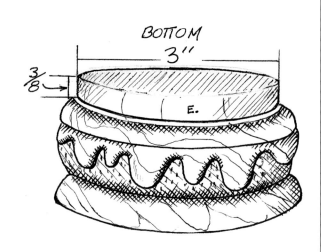

BOTTOM

3"

3/8

E.

D.

1/8

3/8

BENTWOOD BOX WITH TURNED AND
CARVED LID

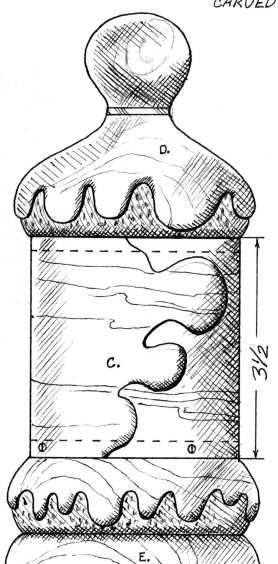

D.

C.

3½

E.

BENTWOOD BOX WITH TURNED
LID

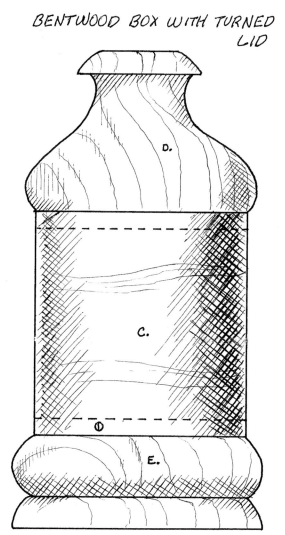

D.

C.

E.

TURNING THE LID
AND THE BOTTOM

1 Screw a faceplate to a band-sawn turning blank with large sheet metal screws. Then, install it on the lathe.

2 This is the same blank after being turned. Above the bead, notice the flange that will fit inside the box's sidewalls.

DECORATING THE SURFACES

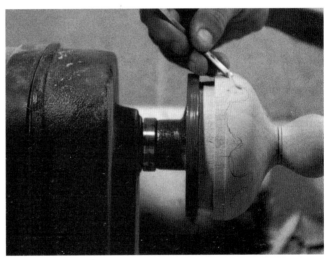

1 Before removing the parts from the lathe, sketch pencil lines on the lid approximating the shapes to be created. Then with gouges of various sweeps, define those lines (shown above).

2 Remove material below the line (as shown above), and create the stippled texture by repeatedly tapping a nail set into the surface of the wood.

MATERIALS LIST			
A	Form	1 pc.	$3 \times 3\frac{1}{2}$
B	Caul	1 pc.	$\frac{1}{2} \times 3\frac{1}{2} \times 3\frac{1}{2}$
C	Sidewall	1 pc.	$\frac{1}{16} \times 3\frac{1}{2} \times 15$
D	Lid	1 pc.	variable
E	Bottom	1 pc.	variable
F	Pegs	4 pc.	$\frac{1}{8} \times \frac{1}{8} \times \frac{1}{2}$

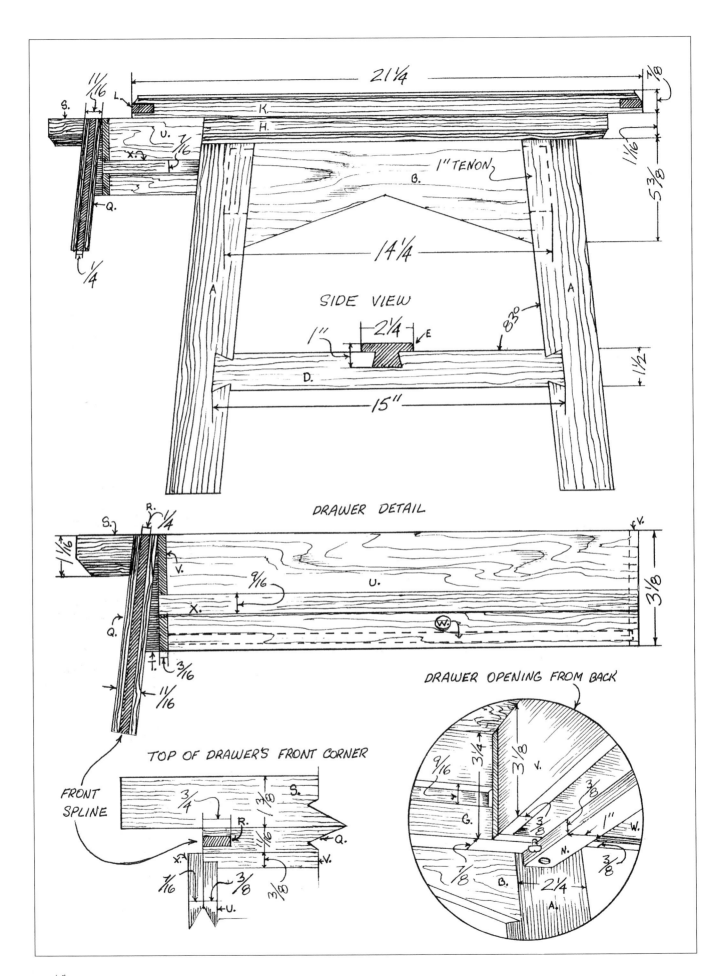

21¼

⁷⁄₈

¹¹⁄₁₆

S.

L.

K.

H.

U. ¹⁄₁₆

X.

Q.

¼

1" TENON

B.

14¼

¹⁄₁₆

5⅜

A.

A.

8°

SIDE VIEW

1"

2¼

E

D.

1½

15"

DRAWER DETAIL

R. ¼

S.

V.

¹⁄₁₆

9⁄₁₆

U.

X.

W.

Q.

T. ³⁄₁₆

¹¹⁄₁₆

V.

3⅛

DRAWER OPENING FROM BACK

FRONT SPLINE

TOP OF DRAWER'S FRONT CORNER

¾

³⁄₁₀₀

S.

R.

¹¹⁄₁₆

Q.

V.

X.

¹⁄₁₆

³⁄₈

³⁄₁₀₀

U.

¾

9⁄₁₆

³⁄₁₀₀

V.

G.

³⁄₈

³⁄₈

1"

W.

N.

³⁄₈

⁷⁄₈

B.

2¼

A.

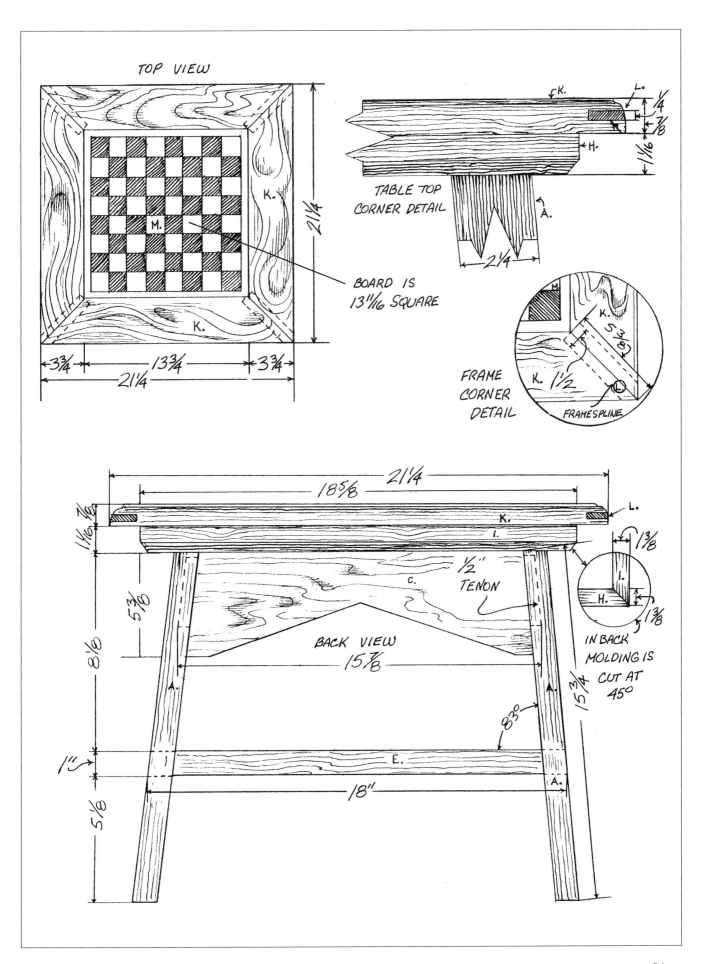

TOP VIEW

M.

BOARD IS
13 11/16 SQUARE

21 1/4

3 3/4   13 3/4   3 3/4
21 1/4

K.

TABLE TOP
CORNER DETAIL

K.   L.   1/4   7/8
H.   1/16

2 1/4   A.

FRAME
CORNER
DETAIL

M   K.   5 3/8
K. 1 1/2
FRAME SPLINE

21 1/4
18 5/8

K.   L.
I.
1/16 7/8

c.   1/2"
TENON

5 3/8

8 1/8

BACK VIEW
15 7/8

A.   A.   15 3/4

83°

1 3/8
I.
H.   1 3/8

IN BACK
MOLDING IS
CUT AT
45°

1"
E.
18"   A.

5 1/8

chapter six for a photo of this jig in operation. Please note, however, that in order to cut the slots for the splines on the frame of the chess table, the work would be aligned so that the mitered end of the frame stock sets flat on the saw table). Thickness and cut splines, and assemble the frame.

Next, install the ¼″ chessboard base in its ¼″ × ½″ rabbet with a number of small wood screws.

The moulding under the tabletop is not merely decorative—it's also functional, serving to fasten the top to the base via a number of wood screws passing up through the moulding into the top and passing through the apron into the moulding.

The drawer is a simple open-topped, butt-jointed box, to the front end of which a section of the apron and the moulding are affixed so that when the drawer is closed,

both the apron and the moulding appear to run continuously around the table. Place a wedge of wood the full length of the drawer front, tapered from a bottom thickness of ⁵⁄₁₆″ to a top thickness of 0 between the drawer front and the apron that covers the drawer front. This shim causes the apron to be canted at the same 83° angle as the other sections of the apron. Slide the runners screwed to the outside faces of the drawer sides into the grooves ploughed in the drawer guides. Construct a drawer stop by screwing a strip of wood across the bottom of the drawer guides. When the drawer is opened to its greatest extension, a pair of screws turned slightly into the bottom edge of the drawer sides strike this strip, preventing the drawer from coming out too far and spilling its contents.

After finishing the table, set the chessboard into place on a felt pad.

1 Fasten the stretcher to the leg with a hand-cut dovetail.

2 Screws passing up through this moulding into the top and passing through the apron into the moulding hold the top to the base.

3 Fasten the drawer runner, which slides in the groove ploughed in the drawer guides, to the drawer via several wood screws passing through the drawer side into the slide. Note the shim between the drawer front and the apron. This causes the apron to be canted at the same angle as the table's legs. Note also the spline set into the end grain of the apron. This prevents the corners of the apron from breaking off because of the grain runout on the apron's triangular tips.

4 The drawer can be seen sliding in the groove ploughed in the drawer guide. When the screw turned into the bottom of the drawer side strikes the stop strip, the drawer is prevented from being pulled completely from the table.

4

FOUR-BOARD BENCH

Hickory

The four-board bench, consisting of a top, two legs, and a stretcher, is a classic piece of primitive furniture, which provides low-cost (although not, perhaps, comfortable) seating for several individuals at once. This bench, patterned after one made at the South Union Shaker community and described by John Kassay in *The Book of Shaker Furniture*, is typical of the genre in this regard. Its joinery, however, is atypical, being much more elegantly conceived than is common in rough, country examples.

The legs and stretcher are fastened together with edge cross-lap joints. The legs and top are secured with double-wedged through tenons passing through a dado cut across the bottom side of the bench top.

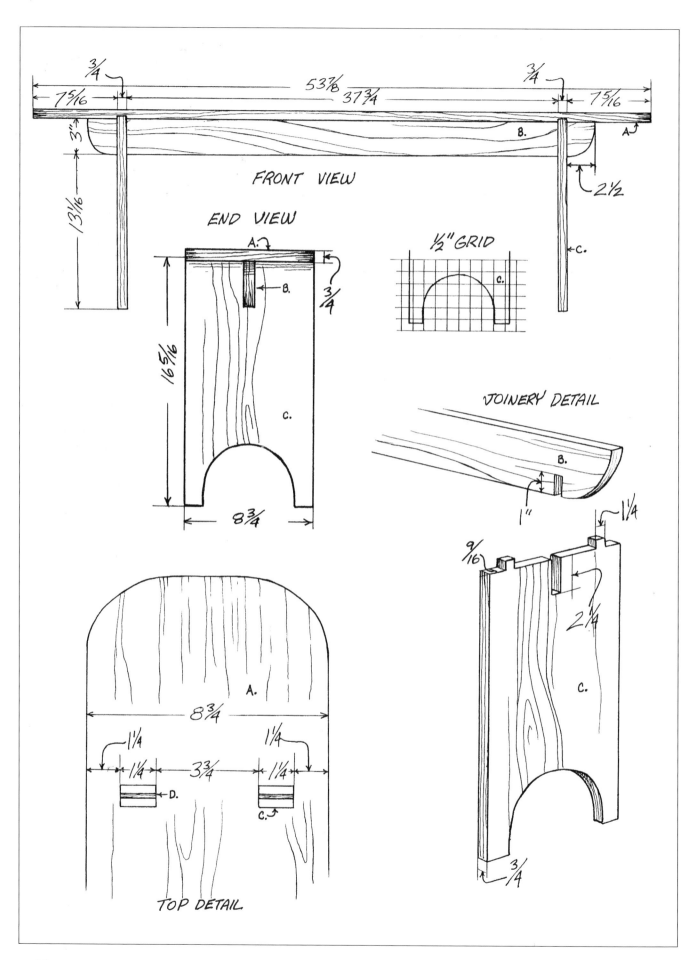

FRONT VIEW

END VIEW

½" GRID

JOINERY DETAIL

TOP DETAIL

MAKING THE FOUR-BOARD BENCH

After the material has been dimensioned, profile the rounded ends of the top, the half round ends on the stretcher, and the circle cutouts on the legs. This can be done on the band saw, but because of the length of the top, it is probably easier to cut this, at least, with a handheld jigsaw.

Next, using a cutoff box on the table saw (or crowded against the fence of the radial arm saw), form the dadoes on the underside of the top. Cut the through mortises cut using the method described in chapter twelve.

Then, on the band saw, cut the through tenons at the tops of the legs. Because of the ¼"-deep dado, these need only be ⁹⁄₁₆" long (½" for the tenon and ¹⁄₁₆" to be sanded flush). Then, fit them into their mortises.

Next, cut the edge cross lap joints that will fasten the stretcher to the legs. Two notches are required at each leg. Cut one, 2¼" deep, in the leg panel midway between the through tenons. Cut the other, 1" deep, into the bottom edge of the stretcher. The extra ¼" in the total depth of the two notches is necessary because of the ¼" dado on the underside of the bench top.

Then cut the notches in the ends of the through tenons using a fine-toothed backsaw. Drill a ⅛" hole from end to end at the base of each notch. This will prevent the tenon from splitting when the wedge is driven into the notch.

After the parts have been dry-fit, glue the joints and assemble the bench.

MATERIALS LIST			
A	Top	1 pc.	¾ × 8¾ × 53⅞
B	Stretcher	1 pc.	¾ × 3 × 44¼
C	Leg	2 pcs.	¾ × 8¾ × 16⁵⁄₁₆
D	Wedge	4 pcs.	³⁄₁₆ × 1⅛ × ¾

These are net measurements. A surplus should be added to lengths of through tenons so that they can be sanded flush.

5

TV RISER

Cherry

A friend asked me if I could make something that would allow her TV to sit above her VCR, keeping both on a relatively narrow table. Working together, we came up with a design much like the piece shown here. With this riser, the VCR can sit on the table top and the TV directly above it. The scrollwork conceals a large air space to cool the VCR.

In earlier centuries, American hardwood forests supplied woodworkers with an apparently inexhaustible supply of wide, clear lumber. If a craftsman needed a 15″-wide cherry board, he simply pulled one from the lumber pile. Today, however, the forests that supplied these riches are nearly gone.

Such boards do still exist, and once or twice I have owned examples. But they are rare, and for most projects requiring wide boards, it's necessary to create that width by gluing-up narrower stock. The 15″ width of this TV riser, for example, was made possible by that most basic and most sadly named of the woodworker's techniques: the butt joint.

MAKING THE TV RISER

First, the material that will make up the riser is glued together (this process is discussed in the sidebar on page 33). Then, dress down the glued-up panel to a flat surface and a consistent thickness. In a shop with a big planer, this involves nothing more than feeding the stock into the machine; but in a small shop, like mine, this 15″ panel must be flattened and smoothed with hand planes.

If the boards used to create the panel were all flat and all aligned correctly at glue-up, you may not need to do more than scrape away the glue squeeze-out and make a couple of token passes with a jack plane. However, boards are rarely flat, often undulating along their lengths like bacon. In such cases, more substantial plane work may be needed.

I begin by exchanging the regular iron in my jack plane for one that's been crowned across its width. This shape eliminates the sharp corners on either side of the iron's width, corners that can dig too deeply into the planed surface when the craftsman is attempting to remove material quickly. With this crowned iron, it's relatively easy to remove significant amounts of thickness. It does, however, leave a rippled, rather than smooth, surface, so it must be followed by a plane fit with a conventional iron.

Next, cut the grooves into which the scrollwork will be inset. You can cut the groove across the bottom face of the top panel in one pass over a table saw fit with a ⅜″ stack of dado cutters. But the grooves in the two end panels must be handled differently. Because the scrollwork is only two inches high, stopped grooves are necessary.

You can cut these freehand with a mallet and chisel or start them on the table saw and finish them by hand.

The scroll is then thicknessed, ripped to width, and profiled on the band saw.

Following the procedure discussed in chapter twenty-five, cut the through dovetails joining the end and top panels. Then, glue-up the riser around the strip of scrollwork, and plug the holes in the ends of the grooves.

CUTTING A STOPPED GROOVE ON THE TABLE SAW

1 To match the 2″ height of the scrollwork, the groove must stop 2⅜″ from the top of the end panels. The extra ⅜″ provides for the ¾″ top minus the ⅜″ groove cut into that top.

The arrow penciled on the fence marks a point 2⅜″ past the leading edge of the dado cutters.

2 When the end panel is fed into the cutters as far as the penciled arrow, the cutters have advanced the groove 2⅜″. (Due to the circular shape of the dado cutters, a bit of material will remain in the end of the groove. This is removed with a chisel.)

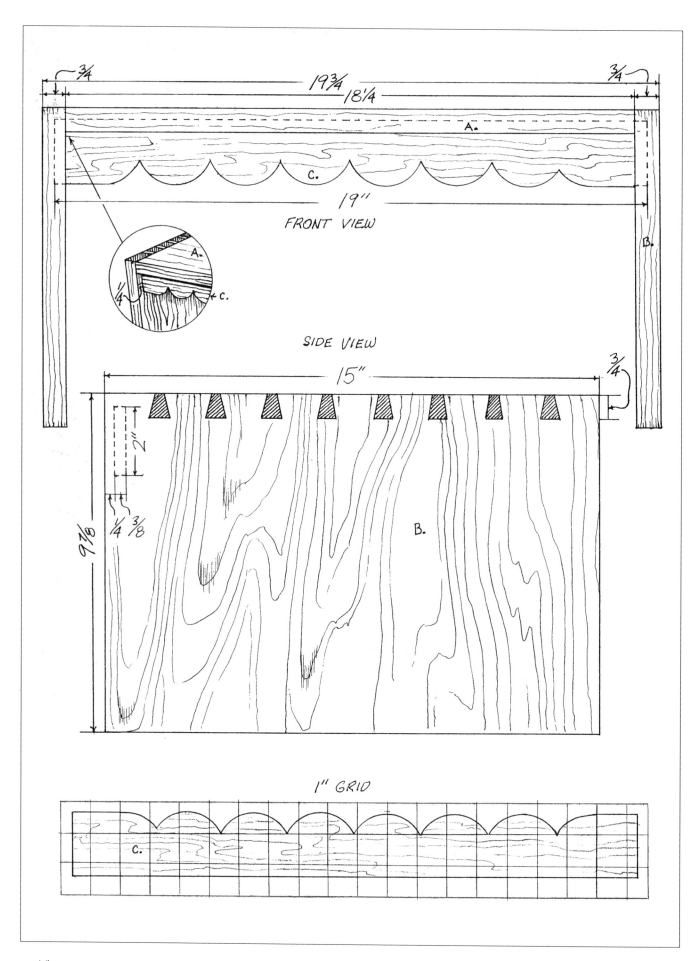

3/4   19 3/4   3/4
18 1/4

A.

C.

19"

FRONT VIEW

B.

A.

1/4   C.

SIDE VIEW

15"   3/4

2"

9 1/8

1/4 3/8

B.

1" GRID

C.

GLUING-UP PANELS

1 Matching figure and color is the first step. Here, two walnut boards with sapwood edges are being matched.

2 These two pieces of cherry were both cut from the same board, assuring a consistent color. Also, making the joint at the edges of the board where the lines of figure cluster close together helps to produce an invisible glue line.

3 A wash of mineral spirits reveals color, enabling you to achieve better matches.

4 Once you have matched (or, as in this case, contrasted) color and grain, form glue joints (the lowly butt joints) on the edges of each board. These joints consist of nothing more than flat, straight planes 90° from the board's adjacent surfaces.

You can create the joint by hand, usng a jack or jointing plane. However, this is fussy work requiring experience and a steady hand. You can also create the joint on the jointer, a stationary power tool designed to perform this very task.

After cutting the joints, coat each edge with glue and align them in pipe or bar clamps. These are necessary in order to bring the joints tightly together.

Clamp arrangement should follow the pattern shown above. Position them no more than 12"-15" apart on alternate sides of the panel. After a couple of hours, you can remove them; within eight hours, you can work the panel.

MATERIALS LIST			
A	Top	1 pc.	¾ × 15 × 19¾
B	End	2 pcs.	¾ × 15 × 9⅞
C	Scroll	1 pc.	⅜ × 2 × 19
D	Plug	2 pcs.	⅜ × ⅜ × ⅜, shaved to fit

These are net measurements. Surplus length should be added to all dovetailed parts to allow them to be sanded flush.

6

SHAKER-STYLE MIRROR

Walnut, Curly Maple

As with several other pieces in this book, I began this mirror with the intent of reproducing a Shaker design. However, the more I studied the drawing of the original in John Kassay's *The Book of Shaker Furniture*, the less I liked certain of its features. Its most appealing detail, the faceted edges at the top of the blade, weren't repeated anywhere else on either the mirror or the blade, so after a little reshaping of the shelf, I brought this faceted edge to the shelf front that holds the bottom of the mirror in place, hoping to make better use of this detail.

I also made other changes. Although the original was constructed of cherry and pine, I chose curly maple and walnut in order to make a more dramatic presentation. Also, the mirror frame stock on the original measured only ½″ × ⅞″, which I thought was little light even for a mirror which would be supported, not by screw eyes turned into its frame, but by a shelf. I decided, then, to increase the dimensions of that frame stock to ¾″ × 1¼″.

MAKING THE SHAKER-STYLE MIRROR

Begin construction with the mirror itself. After thicknessing the frame stock, cut the ½″ × ⅜″ rabbet on what will become the back, inside edge of the frame. (This rabbet will ultimately receive the glass and the glass backing.) Form a radius on the two front edges of the frame stock.

Then miter the frame parts. You can do this on a miter box or a table saw or radial arm saw using a very fine-toothed blade. At this point, cut the slots for the feathers that will later join the frame parts. You can cut these by hand with a tenon saw or on a table saw fit with a hollow-ground planer blade, using a Universal Jig to control the stock as it is passed over the blade. Precision is important in the cutting of both the miters and the feather slots as these joints comprise the entire inventory of joinery in the mirror frame. Any error in these processes is very difficult to hide.

The feather stock is then thicknessed and slid into the slots, marked, and cut. The frame is assembled with glue.

The hanger consists of only three parts: the blade, the shelf and the shelf front.

Fashion the blade first. After cutting its shape on the band saw, facet the top edges. Do this by hand, guided by a marking system similar to that used in the hand manufacture of the raised panel in chapter one. First, draw a line down the center of each edge to be faceted. Then draw lines on the front and back faces of the blade adjacent to these edges. These lines should be placed about ³⁄₁₆″ from the corners. Then, by using a wood file to create planes, join the lines down the center of the edges and the lines

The walnut wedges in the mirror frame corners are not only beautiful, they also add structural support.

on the blade's faces. You could create these planes freehand, but the reference lines make it much easier to produce regular shapes.

Cut a dado on the back edge of the shelf, and position the blade in that dado, holding it there with a bit of glue and two 1½″ no. 12 wood screws.

Then profile the shelf front on the band saw and facet all except the top edges in the same manner as that used for the top edges of the blade. Glue this to the front edge of the shelf.

After sanding and finishing the wood parts, place the mirror glass and a matt board backing inside the rabbet cut in the back side of the mirror frame. Hold both in place with the protruding heads of a half-dozen wood screws turned into the sides of the frame rabbet.

1 Clamp a piece of mitered frame stock in the Universal Jig prior to passing it over the hollow-ground planer blade. Notice that the frame stock rests on its mitered tip and is clamped in the jig at a 45° angle.

2 The faceting at the top of the blade can be seen in this shot. The same faceting is used on all but the top edges of the shelf front.

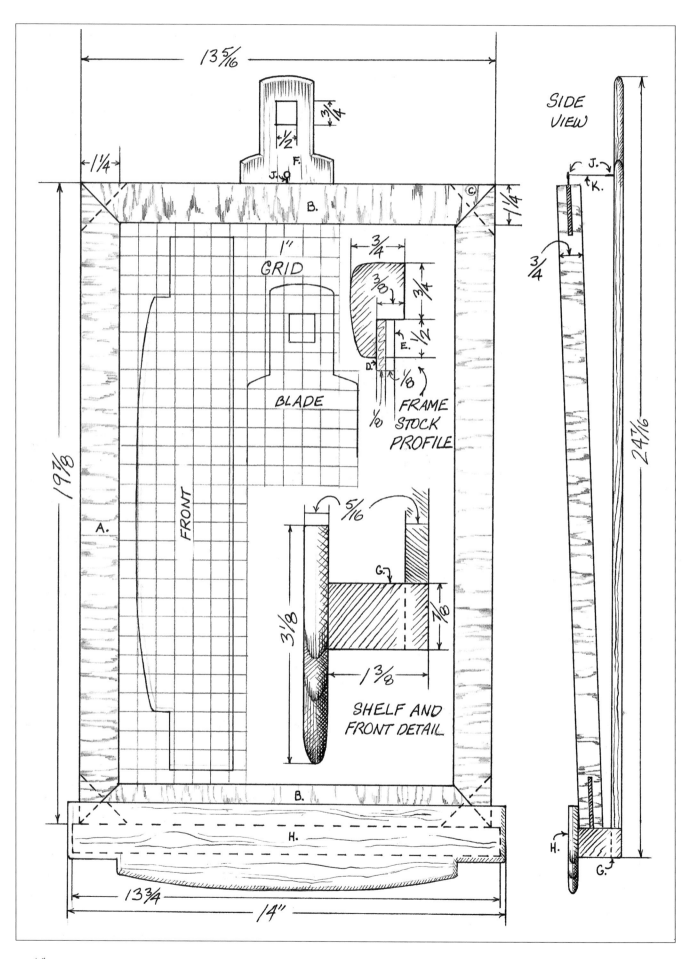

13 5/16

3/4

1/2

F.

1 1/4

J.

B.

C.

1 1/4

1" GRID

3/4

3/8

3/4

1/2

E.

D.

1/8

FRAME STOCK PROFILE

1/8

BLADE

FRONT

A.

19 7/8

5/16

G.

1/16

3 1/8

1 3/8

SHELF AND FRONT DETAIL

B.

H.

13 3/4

14"

SIDE VIEW

J.

K.

3/4

24 1/16

H.

G.

ADHESIVES

A recent *Woodworker's Supply* catalog lists eleven different types of adhesives. Several of those—for example, hot melt glues—are available in different formulas for different applications. These different formulas increase the actual number of choices to sixteen.

Sixteen kinds of glue?

Without devoting significant time to study and experimentation, no woodworker is likely to make the perfect adhesive choice for any particular application. And who wants to spend hours studying adhesives?

In my shop, except for specialized applications (for example bonding Formica-like products to wood), I've reduced the adhesive inventory to three choices: white glue (plain old Elmer's), yellow glue, and hide glue, all of which are more or less appropriate for any wood-to-wood joint.

Each of these three types forms a bond that is stronger than necessary for wood furniture. The primary differences are the amount of working time they allow, the ease with which joints they've bonded can be disassembled, and the convenience of their application.

Hide glue allows for relatively easy disassembly when making repairs and also offers the woodworker the longest working time. It's available in two forms, each of which, unfortunately, has its own set of drawbacks. Traditional hide glue, which comes in flakes or pearls, must be mixed with water and kept heated to a temperature of 140-150° F. Then, after a few days, it must be thrown out and a new batch mixed because, once mixed and heated, it quickly loses its strength. All of this is a significant inconvenience for the owner of a small shop.

The other form comes premixed in squeeze bottles just like white and yellow glues. Unfortunately, however, its shelf life is shorter than white or yellow glue and much shorter than the dry form of hide glue.

In terms of convenience, both white and yellow glue are clearly superior to hide glue. They come premixed in easy-to-use squeeze bottles. They have long shelf life if kept from freezing, and they form an all-but-unbreakable bond between two pieces of joined wood.

There are, however, drawbacks to their use. First, because the bond they form is all-but-unbreakable, a piece assembled with these glues is very difficult to repair. If a yellow- or white-glue-assembled chair comes into my shop needing a new rung, I have to explain to the customer that I can't predict the cost of the repair.

MATERIALS LIST			
Mirror			
A Sides	2 pcs.		$\frac{3}{4} \times 1\frac{1}{4} \times 19\frac{7}{8}$
B Top and bottom	2 pcs.		$\frac{3}{4} \times 1\frac{1}{4} \times 13\frac{5}{16}$
C Feather	4 pcs.		$\frac{3}{32} \times 1\frac{1}{8} \times 2\frac{1}{8}$
D Mirror glass	1 pc.		$\frac{1}{8} \times 11\frac{11}{16} \times 18\frac{1}{4}$
E Mirror backing	1 pc.		$\frac{1}{8} \times 11\frac{11}{16} \times 18\frac{1}{4}$
Rack			
F Blade	1 pc.		$\frac{5}{16} \times 3 \times 24\frac{7}{16}$
G Shelf	1 pc.		$\frac{7}{8} \times 1\frac{3}{8} \times 13\frac{3}{4}$
H Front	1 pc.		$\frac{5}{16} \times 3\frac{1}{8} \times 14$
Hardware			
I Brass eye hook	2 pcs.		$\frac{7}{8}$
J Brass chain			
K Screws	various		

Whereas a chair assembled with hide glue can be disassembled by applying warm water to a tight joint, thus allowing a fairly predictable repair time, the same chair assembled with white or yellow glue may resist my best efforts at disassembly. On more than one occasion, I've broken the slab seat on an old Windsor trying to break loose parts that have been joined with white or yellow glue.

The second problem associated with the use of white and yellow glues is short assembly time. When using these products, a woodworker may have only ten or fifteen minutes to get parts aligned and clamped before the glue grabs and adjustments become all but impossible to make. The time constraints applied to the assembly process by white and yellow glues add stress to an already stressful procedure.

In my shop, I follow these guidelines when choosing an adhesive:

1. For large, complex pieces with a high dollar value (pieces for which one could justify the cost of making repairs), I use hide glue.

2. For pieces requiring lengthy assembly time, I use hide glue.

3. For all other applications, I turn to the ease and convenience of white and yellow glues. For example, all the pieces in this book were assembled with one of those two varieties, the choice being determined by the proximity of the glue bottle to my hand when it was time to glue something up.

7

SIDE TABLE WITH CURLY MAPLE DRAWER

Cherry, Curly Maple

Like many Hepplewhite-style tables, this piece has legs tapering on the inside edges from floor to apron. However, unlike any Hepplewhite-style tables I've seen, it has dainty turned feet at the ends of each of those tapered legs. The idea isn't mine—it's another of many I stole from the Shakers, but it is, I think, what makes this particular table work.

This table also features the use of cross-band inlay. The drawer front, which is made of curly maple, has two bands of cherry inlaid across its width. The tabletop, which is made of cherry, has two inlaid bands of curly maple across its width. It was my hope that this technique would allow me to include a curly maple drawer front as part of an otherwise cherry table.

MAKING THE SIDE TABLE
WITH CURLY MAPLE DRAWER

Joint, glue and clamp the boards selected for the top and set aside. Next, fashion the legs.

Rip and joint the leg stock to 1″ × 1″, and draw the tapers on the front and side of each leg. At the base of the apron, these two faces measure the full 1″ × 1″. At the floor, the legs measure $\frac{9}{16}$″ × $\frac{9}{16}$″. Then cut the tapers on the band saw, keeping the blade well to the waste sides of the taper lines. Finish the taper with a hand plane, while holding the stock in a vise.

Next, center the leg stock so that it can be loaded into the lathe prior to turning the feet. On the narrow end of each leg, this is simply a matter of drawing diagonals across the end grain. On the other end of the leg, however, finding the center is a bit more complicated because you don't want the actual center of the 1″ × 1″ end grain square. What you do want is the center of the $\frac{9}{16}$″ × $\frac{9}{16}$″ end grain square directly in line with the square on the opposite end of the leg. To find this, draw a square measuring $\frac{9}{16}$″ × $\frac{9}{16}$″ on the end grain with two sides of that square directly on top of what will become the outside edges of that leg. Draw diagonals on this square to find the center.

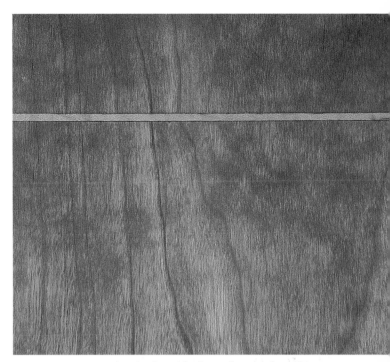

The thin contrasting band inlay adds the perfect touch to this tabletop.

1 The table's dainty turned foot is blended into the flat, tapered sides.

Then mount the leg in the lathe. In order to eliminate the fraying of corners that can occur when a round shape is turned immediately adjacent to a square shape along the length of a turned part, relieve the four corners of the leg with a knife just above the turned foot. Blend this cut into the round tip of the leg with a lathe tool. Finally, clean up with a chisel, knife and sandpaper.

Next, cut the mortises that will receive the tenons on the ends of the apron parts and drawer rails. Set these so that the outside faces of the apron parts are recessed $\frac{1}{8}$″ from the outside faces of the legs. Set the drawer rails, however, so that their outside faces are flush with the outside faces of the legs. When the mortises are fit, assemble the table frame. Next, install drawer runners and kicker strips. Fit the kicker strips with oversized holes, through which screws will pass into the top. The oversized holes allow for expansion and contraction across the width of the top in response to seasonal changes in humidity.

Next, make the drawer. Construction is standard, with through dovetails at the back and half-blind dovetails at the front.

After leveling and smoothing the top (see chapter five), the top and drawer front are inlaid. This process, which is covered in chapter seventeen, is built around the capabilities of the hollow-ground planer blade.

Affix the top to the table frame, turn a pull from a bit of cherry scrap, and sand and finish the table.

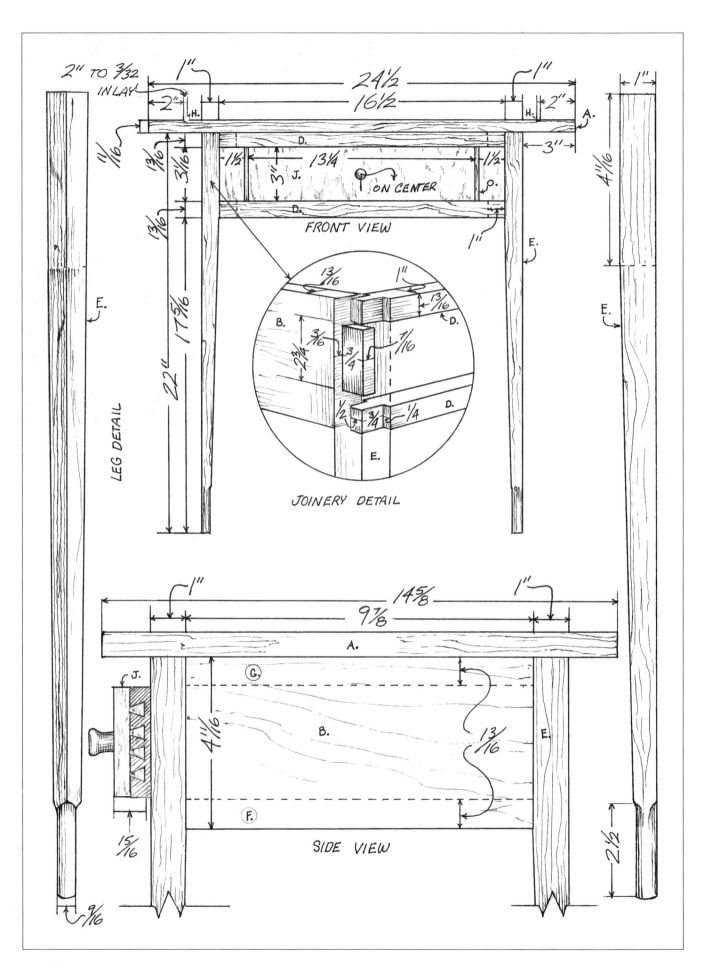

2" TO 3/32 INLAY

1"

24½
16½

1"

1"

2"

H.

H.

2"

A.

3"

1"

4 11/16

1 1/16

13/16

3 3/16

13/16

D.

1½

13¼

1½

3"

J.

ON CENTER

O.

D.

E.

FRONT VIEW

E.

22"   17 5/16

LEG DETAIL

E.

13/16

1"

13/16

D.

B.

3/16

3/4

1/16

2¾

2¼

3/4

1/2

3/4

1/4

D.

E.

JOINERY DETAIL

1"

14 5/8

1"

9 7/8

A.

J.

C.

4 11/16

B.

13/16

E.

F.

15/16

SIDE VIEW

2½

9/16

2 A strip of cherry is inlaid across the width of the drawer's curly maple front. Similarly, a strip of curly maple is inlaid across the width of the table's cherry top. Note the peg driven into the tenon of the drawer rail below the drawer front.

MATERIALS LIST			
Table			
A	Top	1 pc.	$^{11}/_{16} \times 14^{5}/_{8} \times 24^{1}/_{2}$
B	Apron side	2 pcs.	$^{13}/_{16} \times 4^{11}/_{16} \times 11^{3}/_{8}$
C	Apron back	1 pc.	$^{13}/_{16} \times 4^{11}/_{16} \times 18$
D	Drawer rail	2 pcs.	$^{13}/_{16} \times 1 \times 18*$
E	Leg	4 pcs.	$1 \times 1 \times 22$
F	Drawer runner	2 pcs.	$^{13}/_{16} \times 1 \times 9^{7}/_{8}$
G	Kicker strip	2 pcs.	$^{13}/_{16} \times 1 \times 9^{7}/_{8}$
H	Inlay	2 pcs.	$^{3}/_{32} \times ^{3}/_{32} \times 14^{5}/_{8}$
I	Screws	various	
Drawer			
J	Front	1 pc.	$^{15}/_{16} \times 3 \times 16^{7}/_{16}$
K	Side	2 pcs.	$^{1}/_{2} \times 3 \times 10$
L	Back	1 pc.	$^{1}/_{2} \times 2^{1}/_{2} \times 16^{7}/_{16}$
M	Bottom	1 pc.	$^{1}/_{2} \times 9^{5}/_{8} \times 15^{15}/_{16}$
N	Pull	1 pc.	$^{5}/_{8} \times 1^{1}/_{4}$
O	Inlay	2 pc.	$^{3}/_{32} \times ^{3}/_{32} \times 3$

Includes ¾" tenons on either end.
These are net measurements. Surplus should be added to dove-tailed parts to allow them to be sanded flush.

8

FOOTSTOOL

Cherry, Walnut, Oak

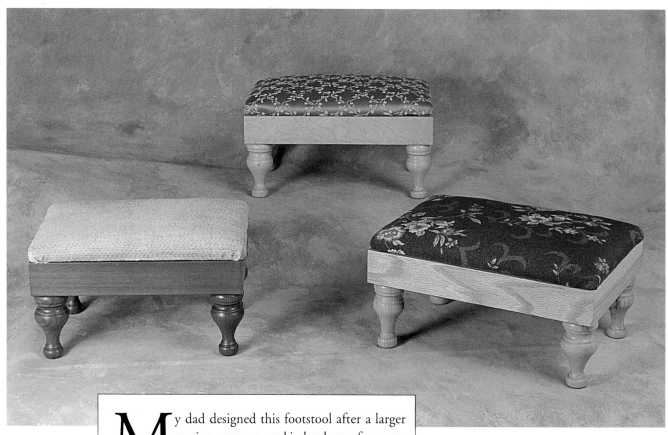

DESIGNED BY
JIM PIERCE

My dad designed this footstool after a larger version my aunt used in her home for many years. The original had a mahogany frame and mahogany legs both stained very dark. The fabric, too, was dark: a needlepoint with a black ground upon which a floral pattern had been rendered.

Since the footstool is small, requiring little material (many of the parts are small enough to be made from scrap), he decided to do a limited production run to take greater advantage of the machine setups for cutting glue blocks, screw strips, and the mitered and splined frame. As a result, he produced a dozen copies in much less than twelve times the hours it would have taken to produce one.

MAKING THE FOOTSTOOL

Construction begins with the legs since they are the most time-consuming components. Rip out 2 × 2 stock, cut to length, and center on the lathe. First, turn the ½″ × ⅞″ tenon on the top of the leg. Care must be taken in sizing the tenon so that a tight fit can be achieved. In my shop, I begin tenon sizing with a gouge, reducing the stock to ¹⁄₁₆″ over its finished diameter. Then, with a flat (paring) chisel laid bevel side down on the tool rest, I bring the tenon to its final size, checking frequently with calipers. (Charles Harvey, a chairmaker in Berea, Kentucky, uses an open-end wrench to check tenon diameter.)

After sizing the tenon, give the leg its rough shape. Then form the coves and beads.

The frame is next. After dimensioning the stock, cut miters on each end of the frame components. Then, on a table saw fit with a ¼″ stack of dado cutters tilted to a 45° angle, cut the dado for the spline on each end of every mitered piece.

Then rip out spline stock to a width of 2¹⁄₁₆″. Thickness to ¼″. When you have achieved a tight fit in the dadoes, crosscut the individual splines from the length of spline stock. Remember that the grain of the finished spline must run perpendicular to the mitered faces of the pieces being joined.

This photo shows the structural parts of the stool.

Assemble the splined and mitered frame. When the glue has dried, glue the triangular glue blocks in each corner and screw them into place. Take exact measurements for the screw strips and cut and install the strips.

The top of the footstool is a piece of ⅝″ wood stock on which a piece of ½″ foam padding has been placed. This is held in place by upholstery cloth wrapped around the top and stapled underneath.

Turn four screws up through the screw strips into the bottom side of the top to hold it in place.

AIR-DRYING LUMBER

Lumber is expensive.

Beautiful lumber is very expensive.

In Central Ohio, where I live, it's not unusual to find prices of $5 a board foot on FAS cherry. (FAS refers to Firsts and Seconds, the best available grade.) Walnut is even more expensive.

One way to avoid these high prices is to switch from the expensive kiln-dried lumber available at retail outlets to the much less expensive green lumber available at sawmills. Preparing green lumber for use does require labor and time, but the cash savings can be enormous. In my area, I never pay more than $2 a board foot for green FAS cherry—sometimes I can get it for less.

You can realize even greater savings if you are willing to take down the trees and hire someone with a portable sawmill to come to the site and saw the logs into boards. (This is discussed in *Woodwork* issue no. 33.) In my area, the price for such custom sawing ranges from $.20 to $.35 per foot. Of course, no log yields 100 percent

FAS, but most will yield some, and there is much usable material in the cheaper common grades, particularly when the pieces to be built (like the projects in this book) are modest in size.

Before the green lumber can be air-dried, a solid foundation for the drying pile must be built.

First, you must choose an acceptable location. Drying piles are not beautiful things. For that reason a backyard might be a better choice than a front yard. Air movement is also important. The site should also be open enough so that wind can blow through the pile to aid in reducing the moisture content. Finally, it should be situated on a slight grade so that water can run off whatever roofing material is placed atop the pile.

Begin the foundation with six concrete blocks set in two parallel rows of three. Set these so that the length of each row (measured from outside to outside of the end blocks) is about 8′. Again, measured from outside to outside, place the rows about 4′ apart. Make some

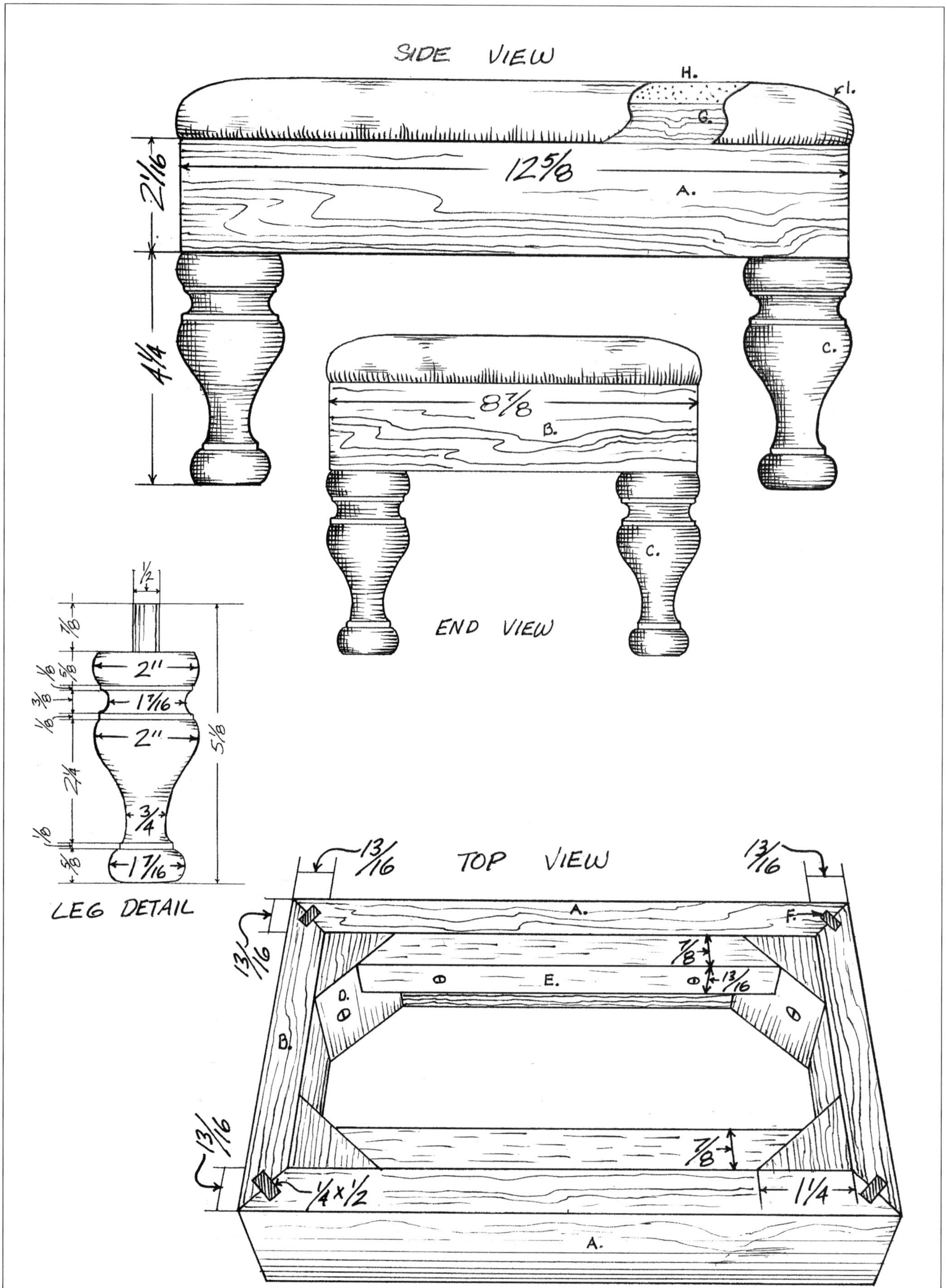
SIDE VIEW
H.
I.
G.
2 1/16
12 5/8
A.
4 1/4
C.
8 7/8
B.
C.
END VIEW
1/2
7/8
1/8
5/8
2"
3/8
1 7/16
1/8
2"
5 1/8
2 1/4
3/4
1/8
5/8
1 7/16
LEG DETAIL
13/16
TOP VIEW
13/16
A.
F.
13/16
7/8
E.
13/16
D.
B.
13/16
7/8
1/4 x 1/2
1 1/4
A.

effort to get the tops of these blocks into the same plane. Later, you can use shimming to correct minor inaccuracies.

Next, lay a row of railroad ties along each row of three blocks. Set these so that their top surfaces are in the same plane. You can check this by sighting across the ties from the side, shimming where necessary.

Then, set five 4' lengths of 4×4 across the ties at 20"-24" intervals. Again, these must be in the same plane because any twist in the foundation will be transferred to the drying lumber, in some cases making it unusable. Sight along the length of the pile from either end to reveal any twist in the alignment of the top surfaces of the 4×4s.

Air-drying lumber requires a large quantity of stickers, sometimes called sticks. These are nothing more than 1"×1"×48" dry hardwood rips which separate the layers of drying lumber so that air can pass freely through the pile.

Once you have ripped out the stickers, the actual lumber pile can be constructed. First, place a single 1"×1"×48" sticker along the center line of each 4×4 support. Then, place a layer of green lumber perpendicular to and atop that first layer of stickers. As you are laying out these boards, take care so that an air space (approximately 1") is left between the edges of the boards.

MATERIALS LIST			
A Side	2 pcs.	$^{13}/_{16} \times 2^{1}/_{16} \times 12^{5}/_{8}$	
B End	2 pcs.	$^{13}/_{16} \times 2^{1}/_{16} \times 8^{7}/_{8}$	
C Leg	4 pcs.	$2 \times 2 \times 5^{1}/_{8}$	
D Glue block	4 pcs.	$1^{1}/_{4} \times 2^{1}/_{16} \times 2^{5}/_{8}$	
E Screw strip	2 pcs.	$^{13}/_{16} \times ^{7}/_{8} \times 8^{7}/_{8}$, length to fit	
F Spline	4 pcs.	$^{1}/_{4} \times 2^{1}/_{16} \times ^{1}/_{2}$	
G Top	1 pc.	$^{5}/_{8} \times 8^{7}/_{8} \times 12^{5}/_{8}$	
H Foam	1 pc.	$^{1}/_{2} \times 8^{7}/_{8} \times 12^{5}/_{8}$	
I Fabric	1 pc.	14×18	
J Screws	various		

When that first layer of lumber has been positioned, place a second set of stickers across that layer directly above the first row of stickers. Then add a second layer of lumber, followed by another set of stickers and another layer of boards and so on until you have stickered all the green lumber.

Professional driers often build these piles to a height of 12'-14', but I find that if the top of the pile is more than five or six feet above the ground, it becomes too difficult to get the lumber up and down.

Complete the pile with a water-shedding top. It

This photo shows the drying pile beside my shop. Notice that the two railroad ties are positioned on a foundation of concrete blocks. Notice, too, that the roofing material consists of nothing more than a tarp weighted down with scrap wood and bricks.

doesn't need to be fancy. A couple of sheets of roofing metal will do, as will a tarp, or even a layer of knotted and checked lumber—anything that will keep water from percolating down through the pile.

Now, wait. The traditional rule-of-thumb states that material should air-dry outdoors one year for each inch of its thickness. I usually exceed that time allotment, although on a couple of occasions, in a pinch, I brought lumber inside after only six months. However, those six-months did include the prime drying seasons of summer and fall.

After air-drying outdoors, you can take the lumber to a commercial kiln for finish drying or bring it inside and sticker it again in a warm, dry room for a few additional months (this is what I do).

It's then ready to use.

Much has been written about the importance of using kiln-dried material, and retail outlets often brag about the fact that the moisture content of their stock has been reduced to 7 percent.

I think this is misleading. Yes, the lumber might have had a moisture content of 7 percent on the day it was taken from the kiln. But wood is not an inert medium. After leaving the kiln, its moisture content immediately begins the process of moving toward a point of equilibrium with the relative humidity of the surrounding air.

That means that if a craftsman took that 7 percent board to his shop in Death Valley, California, that 7 percent would soon become 4 percent or 3 percent. And if I took that same 7 percent board to my shop in central Ohio during the steamy month of July, that 7 percent moisture content would quickly become 11 percent or 12 percent, which is the same as the moisture content of the material I've prepared for use by air-drying.

The 1″ × 1″ stickers are arranged perpendicular to the layers of drying boards. These stickers provide a space through which air can move to hasten the drying process.

9
TRESTLE TABLE
Walnut

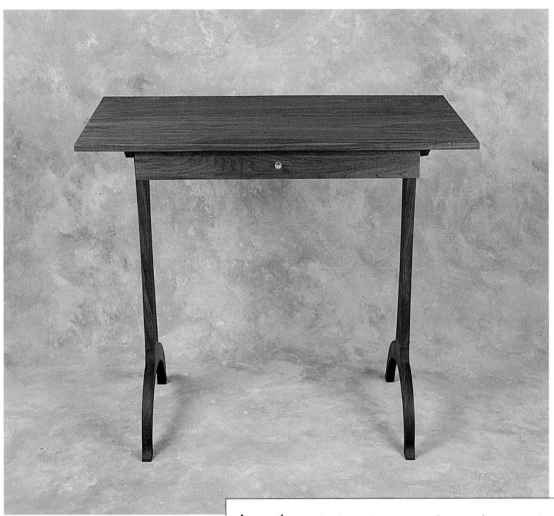

DESIGNED BY
JIM PIERCE

The underslung drawers on the two-drawer sewing stand featured in chapter fourteen have runners screwed to the drawer sides, runners which slide in rabbets cut into the sides of the cleats which hold the table's top flat. The underslung drawer on this trestle table offers an interesting variation on that theme. Instead of runners fastened to the drawer sides, this table features runners fastened to the table frame. The drawer sides, then, have grooves ploughed in their outside faces that slide on these runners.

The original of this table, drawn by John Kassay in *The Book of Shaker Furniture*, was built in the Harvard community of Shakers during the first half of the nineteenth century. Although constructed with sound joinery, it is a delicate piece that could not be put to heavy use.

10

TEN-DRAWER CHEST

Curly Maple, Cherry, Walnut

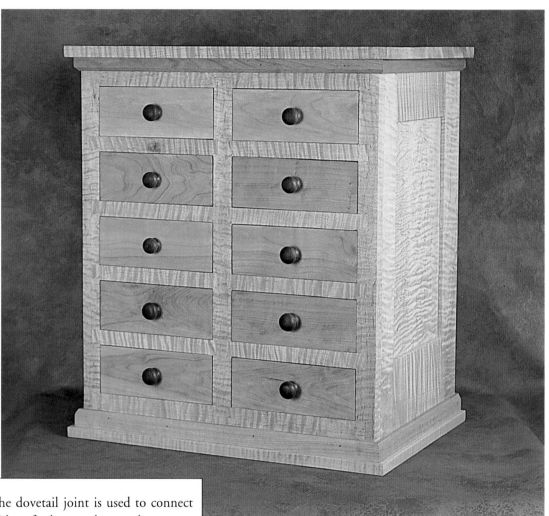

Typically, the dovetail joint is used to connect the four sides of a box, a chest, a drawer—work for which the joint is wonderfully adapted, offering not only extensive glue surface but also mechanical resistance to separation. Less typically, the joint is used in a number of other settings, for exactly the same reasons.

This ten-drawer chest features a face frame assembled with hand-cut dovetail joints. These lock together all the parts of the frame, and they provide a visually complex surface, attracting the eye, delighting it with the intricacies of its jigsaw-puzzle patterns.

DESIGNED BY
JIM PIERCE

MAKING THE TEN-DRAWER CHEST

After the material has been dimensioned, glue-up the top panel and set it aside.

Then cut joints for the face frame. When these have been fit, glue the frame.

Build the end panels next. Because of the seasonal expansion and contraction that will take place across their width, they are built as framed panels with the tongues on the perimeter of the central panel floating in grooves cut into the inside edges of the frame components, which are held together with mortise-and-tenon joinery.

After the end panels have been glued-up, cut dadoes across their width for the tongues on the ends of the dust panels. Then, glue the front edges of the end panels to the back of the face frame.

Assemble the interior of the case in layers beginning at the bottom. First slide the tongues on the bottom dust panel into the dadoes cut on the inside faces of the end panels. Glue and clamp the front edge of the dust panel to the back side of the face frame. After removing the clamps, install the drawer guides and stops for the bottom tier of drawers.

Then, slide the next dust panel into position, glue and clamp it, and install its drawer guides and stops. Continue up the chest until each layer of interior work is completed.

After installing the filler strip at the bottom back of the cabinet, fasten the four mitered sides of the bottom frame in place with screws passing up into the bottom of the end panels and face frame.

Assemble the top frame, with kicker strips, as a separate unit. Before installing it in the cabinet, fasten the top to the frame with screws passing up through slotted screw holes. These holes allow the top to expand and contract across its width in response to seasonal changes in humidity.

Set the top frame, with the top attached, into place. Hold it there with screws passing through the top of the face frame and the tops of the end panels. Nail on the upper moulding, concealing these screws. Nail the lower moulding into place. Drawer construction is straightforward, with through dovetails at the back of the drawers and half-blind dovetails at the front.

MATERIALS LIST

Case

A	Top	1 pc.	$1\frac{1}{16} \times 15\frac{13}{16} \times 21\frac{5}{8}$
B	Short bottom frame	2 pcs.	$1\frac{1}{16} \times 1\frac{11}{16} \times 15\frac{13}{16}$
C	Long bottom frame	2 pcs.	$1\frac{1}{16} \times 1\frac{11}{16} \times 21\frac{5}{8}$
D	Central end panel	2 pcs.	$\frac{5}{8} \times 10\frac{1}{8} \times 14\frac{7}{8}$ [1]
E	Top of end panel frame	2 pcs.	$\frac{7}{8} \times 3\frac{5}{8} \times 10\frac{5}{8}$ [2]
F	Bottom of end panel frame	2 pcs.	$\frac{7}{8} \times 5\frac{3}{16} \times 10\frac{5}{8}$ [2]
G	Back of end panel frame	2 pcs.	$\frac{7}{8} \times 2\frac{15}{16} \times 22\frac{11}{16}$
H	Front of end panel frame	2 pcs.	$\frac{7}{8} \times 2\frac{1}{8} \times 22\frac{11}{16}$
I	Back planking	various	$\frac{1}{2} \times$ various $\times 22\frac{11}{16}$
J	Short upper moulding	2 pcs.	$\frac{5}{16} \times \frac{13}{16} \times 15\frac{7}{16}$
K	Long upper moulding	1 pc.	$\frac{5}{16} \times \frac{13}{16} \times 20\frac{3}{4}$
L	Short lower moulding	2 pcs.	$\frac{3}{8} \times 1\frac{1}{16} \times 15\frac{9}{16}$
M	Long lower moulding	1 pc.	$\frac{3}{8} \times 1\frac{1}{16} \times 20\frac{7}{8}$
N	Outside vertical facing	2 pcs.	$\frac{7}{8} \times 1\frac{1}{4} \times 22\frac{11}{16}$
O	Central vertical facing	1 pc.	$\frac{7}{8} \times 1\frac{1}{4} \times 20$
P	Top horizontal facing	1 pc.	$\frac{7}{8} \times 1\frac{3}{4} \times 18\frac{7}{8}$
Q	Bottom horizontal facing	1 pc.	$\frac{7}{8} \times 2\frac{3}{16} \times 18\frac{7}{8}$
R	Short facing	8 pcs.	$\frac{7}{8} \times \frac{15}{16} \times 9\frac{3}{16}$
S	Dust panel	5 pcs.	$\frac{3}{4} \times 13\frac{3}{4} \times 18\frac{3}{4}$ [3]
T	Drawer stop	10 pcs.	$\frac{3}{16} \times \frac{7}{8} \times 7$
U	Central drawer guide	5 pcs.	$\frac{3}{4} \times 1\frac{1}{16} \times 13\frac{3}{4}$
V	Outside drawer guide	10 pcs.	$\frac{7}{16} \times \frac{7}{8} \times 13\frac{3}{4}$
W	Kicker strip	2 pcs.	$\frac{13}{16} \times 1\frac{5}{8} \times 12\frac{7}{8}$
X	Short top frame	3 pcs.	$\frac{13}{16} \times 1\frac{5}{8} \times 11\frac{1}{4}$
Y	Long top frame	2 pcs.	$\frac{13}{16} \times 1\frac{5}{8} \times 18\frac{1}{4}$
Z	Cleat	1 pc.	$\frac{13}{16} \times 1\frac{5}{8} \times 18\frac{1}{4}$
AA	Bottom filler strip	1 pc.	$\frac{3}{4} \times 1\frac{7}{16} \times 18\frac{1}{4}$

Drawers

BB	Front	10 pcs.	$\frac{1}{4} \times 2\frac{15}{16} \times 8\frac{1}{16}$
CC	Sides	20 pcs.	$\frac{3}{8} \times 2\frac{15}{16} \times 14\frac{1}{8}$
DD	Back	10 pcs.	$\frac{3}{8} \times 2\frac{3}{8} \times 7\frac{15}{16}$
EE	Bottom	10 pcs.	$\frac{5}{16} \times 7\frac{7}{16} \times 14\frac{1}{8}$
FF	Pull	10 pcs.	$1 \times 1\frac{1}{2}$

[1] Includes $\frac{1}{4}" \times \frac{1}{2}"$ tongue on all four edges.
[2] Includes $\frac{3}{4}"$ tenon on each end.
[3] Includes $\frac{1}{4}"$ tongue on each end.
*These are net measurements. Surplus should be added to all dovetailed parts to allow them to be sanded flush.

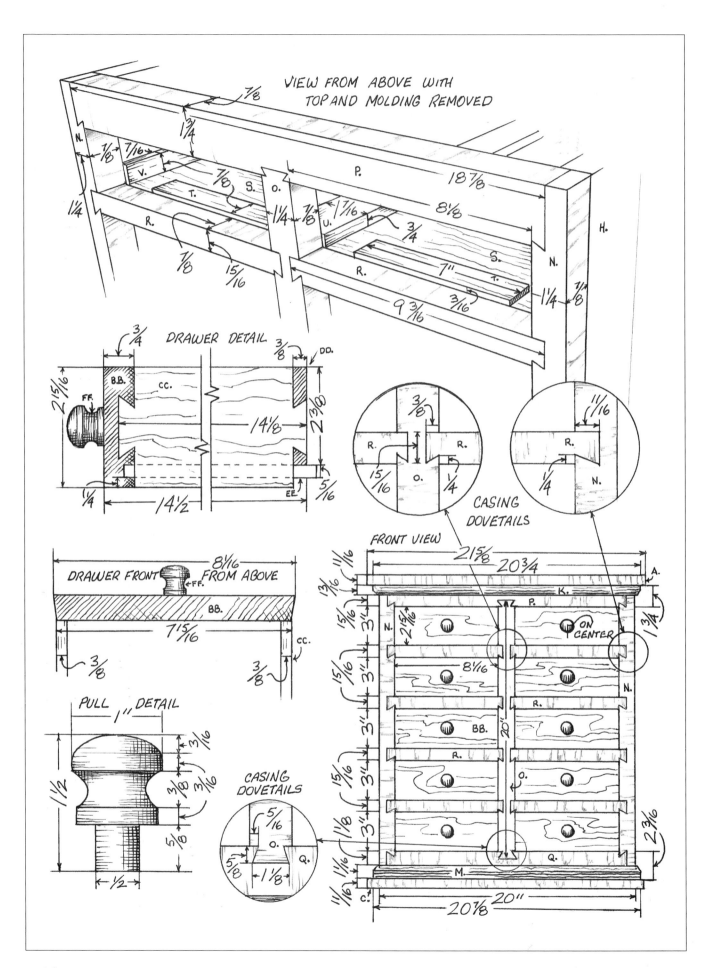

VIEW FROM ABOVE WITH TOP AND MOLDING REMOVED

DRAWER DETAIL

DRAWER FRONT FROM ABOVE

PULL DETAIL

CASING DOVETAILS

CASING DOVETAILS

FRONT VIEW

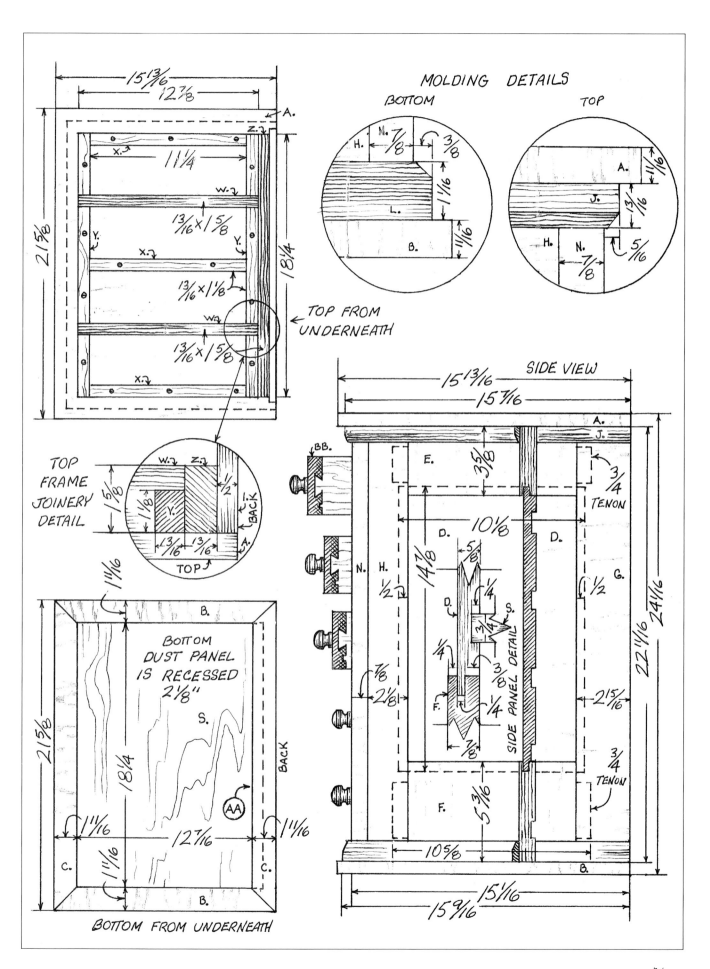

MOLDING DETAILS

BOTTOM

TOP

TOP FROM UNDERNEATH

TOP FRAME JOINERY DETAIL

BOTTOM DUST PANEL IS RECESSED 2⅛"

BOTTOM FROM UNDERNEATH

SIDE VIEW

SIDE PANEL DETAIL

¾ TENON

¾ TENON

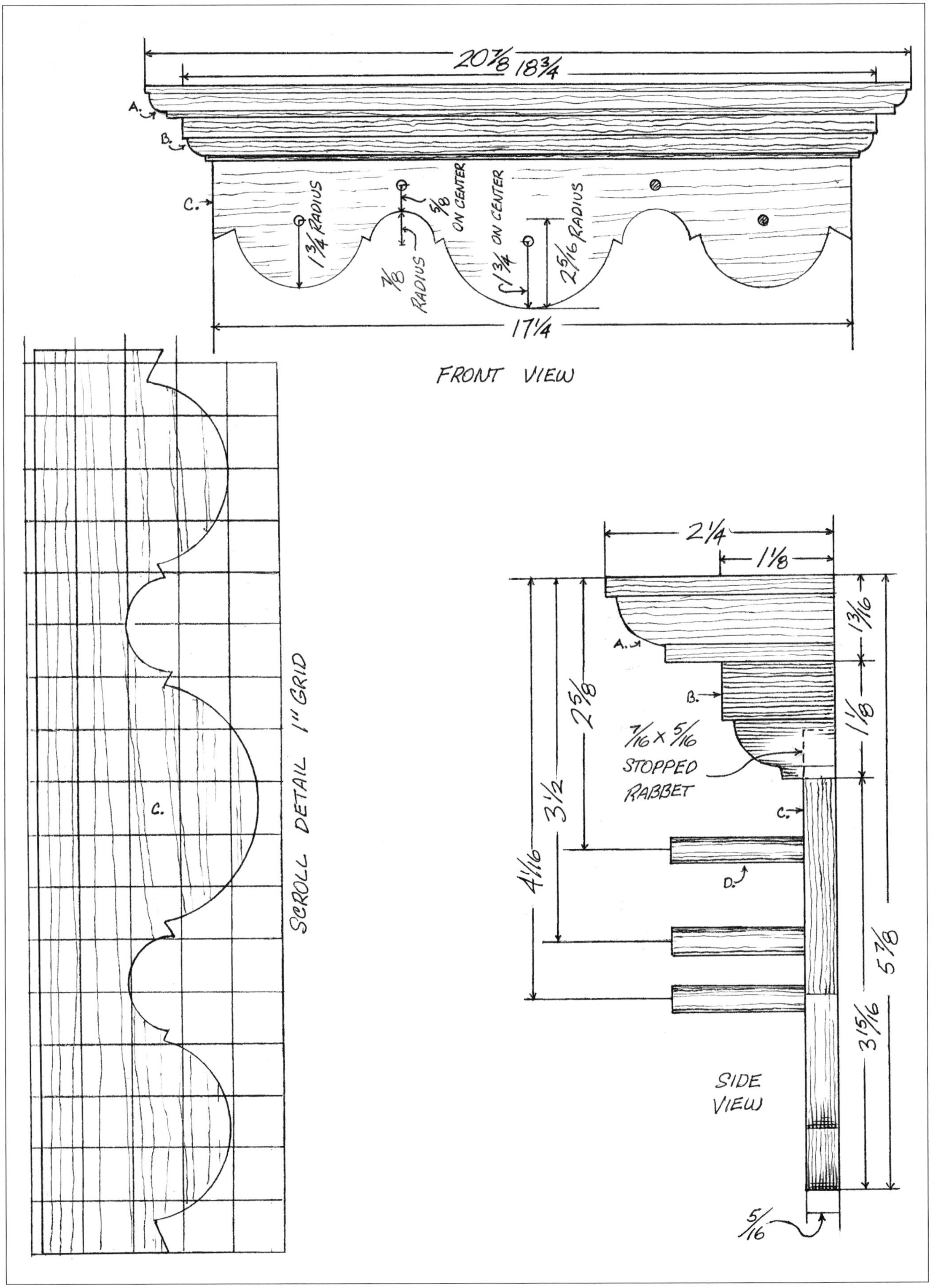

20 7/8
18 3/4
A.
B.
C.
1 3/4 RADIUS
5/8
ON CENTER
1 3/4 ON CENTER
2 5/16 RADIUS
7/8 RADIUS
17 1/4
FRONT VIEW
SCROLL DETAIL 1" GRID
C.
2 1/4
1 1/8
A.
13/16
B.
2 5/8
7/16 x 5/16
STOPPED
RABBET
1 1/8
C.
3 1/2
4 1/16
D.
5 7/8
3 15/16
SIDE VIEW
5/16

will, having been created from the same photoreactive material.

3. **Trust the glue.** Sometimes, no matter how carefully we work, a part will split during a test assembly, but this is rarely the disaster it may at first appear to be.

If the split runs the full length of the part and the two sides can be separated cleanly, a coat of glue on each fractured face and an hour in a set of clamps will restore the part to its original strength.

If the split only runs a couple of inches along the length of a longer piece, you can work glue into the split with a little patience. First, apply a generous layer of glue to the part, directly over the split. Then work the split open and closed a number of times, causing the glue to migrate down into the gap. When it appears that the glue has worked all the way through the split, wash the excess off of the surface, and clamp the part until the glue has cured.

4. **Modify the piece.** In places that can't be reached with shaving tools, I use a wood file to remove band saw marks from scrollwork. In cleaning up the scrollwork for the key rack at the beginning of this chapter, I got a little too aggressive with the file and flaked off some chips from one of the sharp points near the central arc. I worked that point down until I was beyond the torn-out grain, but when I stepped back from the part, I could see that that particular point was visibly different than the other three.

The solution? With a file, I carefully removed enough material from the other three points so that they matched the one on which I'd made my error.

5. **Graft in new material.** While building the figured oak magazine stand (chapter twelve), I got a poor fit on

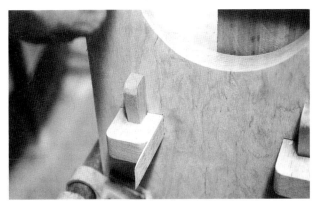

A gap was visible on one side of the tusk tenon so a sliver has been grafted onto the tenon to fill it.

the mortise for one of the eight tusk tenons. The gap was fairly noticeable, and I would have liked to have made a new shelf, but I had no more oak with that particular wavy grain.

To hide the $\frac{1}{16}''$ gap, I ripped a thin sliver from a piece of scrap having grain and color similar to the tusk tenon that fit through the bad mortise. Then, with a C-clamp and a couple of scrap pads, I glued the sliver to the side of the tusk tenon after sliding one end of the sliver into the $\frac{1}{16}''$ gap. When the glue had dried, I cut away the excess and blended the sliver into the curve at the end of the tusk tenon.

The gap hadn't made the joint structurally unsound, and the glued on sliver did conceal the gap, but this wasn't a perfect solution. When that particular tusk tenon is sighted from above, it's clear that there's a little more material on one side of the walnut wedge than there is on the other.

MATERIALS LIST			
A	Shelf	1 pc.	$\frac{13}{16} \times 2\frac{1}{4} \times 20\frac{7}{8}$
B	Mid-section	1 pc.	$1\frac{1}{8} \times 1\frac{1}{8} \times 18\frac{3}{4}$
C	Scroll	1 pc.	$\frac{5}{16} \times 4\frac{3}{8} \times 17\frac{1}{4}$
D	Peg	5 pcs.	$\frac{1}{4} \times 1\frac{5}{8}$
E	Screws		$\frac{3}{4}''$ no. 6

12

FIGURED OAK
MAGAZINE STAND

White Oak, Walnut

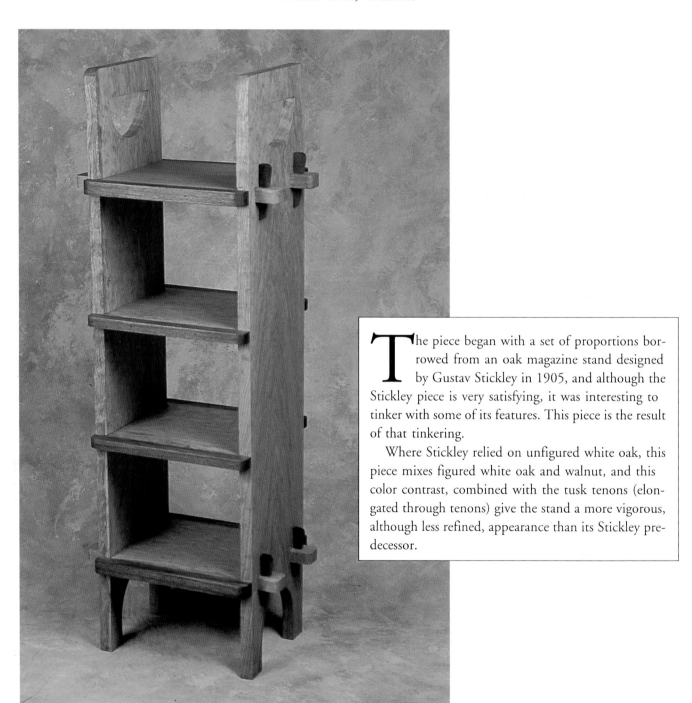

The piece began with a set of proportions borrowed from an oak magazine stand designed by Gustav Stickley in 1905, and although the Stickley piece is very satisfying, it was interesting to tinker with some of its features. This piece is the result of that tinkering.

Where Stickley relied on unfigured white oak, this piece mixes figured white oak and walnut, and this color contrast, combined with the tusk tenons (elongated through tenons) give the stand a more vigorous, although less refined, appearance than its Stickley predecessor.

MAKING THE MAGAZINE STAND

Through tenons completely pierce and, in some cases, extend beyond the outside surface of the board through which they pass. One advantage of this joint over the shorter, more commonly used stopped tenon is increased glue surface.

The through tenon also offers some design opportunities not associated with the stopped tenon. A through tenon can be shaved flush and fit with wedges of contrasting wood, as was done with the through tenons on the ash drying rack pictured in this book (chapter nineteen). Or, as with this magazine stand, the tenons can extend well beyond the outside surface of the board through which they pass and can themselves be given through mortises into which wedges (keys) are driven. These wedges, characteristic of knockdown furniture, provide a mechanical lock for the sides of the case, in addition to adding an appealing visual detail.

After the stock has been thicknessed, ripped to width, and cut to length, lay out and saw the half-circle cutouts that separate the feet and those that form the handgrips with a handheld jigsaw.

Then, cut shelf dadoes. You can do this with a set of dado cutters on the radial arm saw or with a set of cutters on the table saw. At this time, cut the through mortises for the tusk tenons.

Careful marking is essential. First, using a try square, extend the upper and lower limits of the shelf dadoes around the edges and onto the opposite faces of the end panels. These lines mark the upper and lower limits of the through mortises. Then, mark the widths of these mortises and score their perimeters with a knife held against a straightedge.

This wildly figured oak was perfect for this piece.

Remember: Aggressive drilling and chisel work can result in chips breaking out around the perimeter of the mortise on the back side of the board. For this reason, use a backup board during drilling, and lay out the mortise on both sides of the board so you can alternate chisel work from one side to the other, working toward the middle.

After cutting the mortises and fitting the tusk tenons through them, cut the mortises for the walnut wedges. It's important to dry-clamp the whole assembly tightly before marking these mortises so that they will be correctly located along the length of the tusk tenon. Their placement should cause the wedges to draw the case together as they are driven into their mortises. To achieve this, place the inside edge of the wedge mortise so that it will be approximately ⅛" inside the outside face of the end panel at assembly.

When the wedges have been fit, glue and assemble the case, clamping everything tightly together. After the glue has cured, remove the clamps and apply the walnut shelf-facings. Glue and nail these into place (my choice) or glue them and clamp until dry. The second method eliminates the need to fill nail holes, but it is a bit slower.

CUTTING THROUGH MORTISES

1 Careful layout is essential. After marking locations with a pencil, use a knife to score across the grain only on the perimeter of the mortises. This knife line will provide a reliable means for aligning the chisels with which the mortise will be given its final shape.

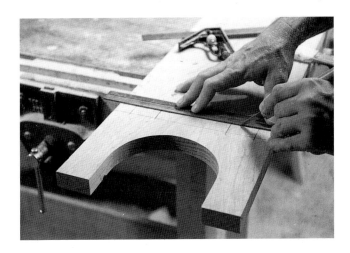

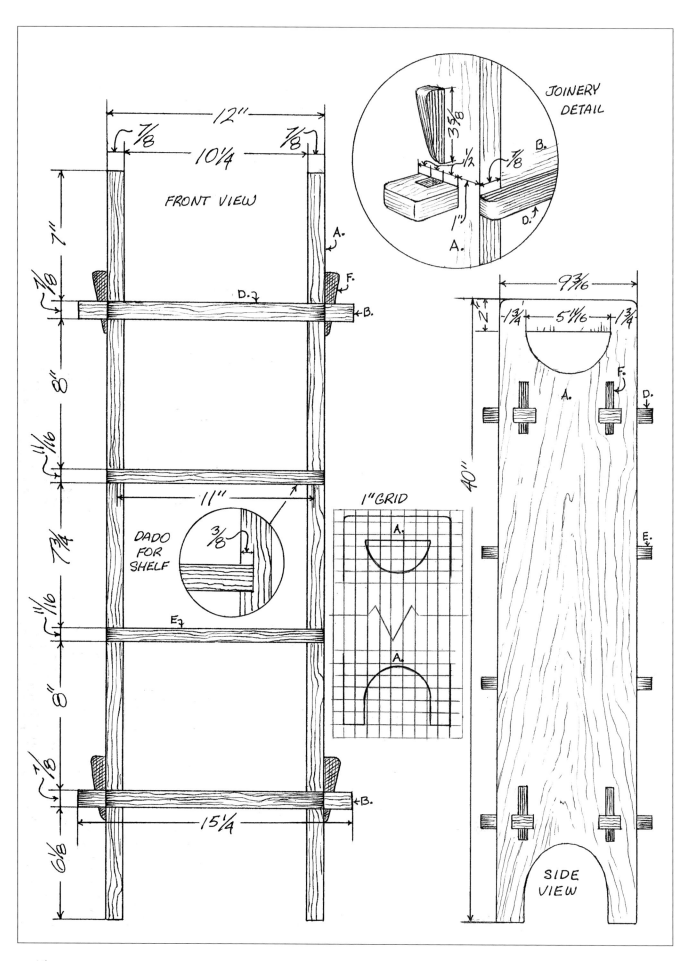

12"

7/8   10 1/4   7/8

FRONT VIEW

7"

1/8

8"

A.

F.

D.

B.

1 1/16

11"

DADO
FOR
SHELF

3/8

7 3/4

E

1 1/16

8"

1/8

15 1/4

B.

6 1/8

JOINERY
DETAIL

3 5/8

1/2   1/8   B.

1"   D.

A.

9 3/16

1 3/4   5 11/16   1 3/4

2"

A.

F.

D.

40"

E.

SIDE
VIEW

1" GRID

A.

A.

CUTTING THROUGH MORTISES (CONTINUED)

2 Then, remove waste with a handheld drill and a Forstner bit.

	MATERIALS LIST		
A	End	2 pcs.	7/8 × 9 3/16 × 40
B	Top and bottom shelf	2 pcs.	7/8 × 9 3/16 × 15 1/4
C	Middle shelf	2 pcs.	11/16 × 9 3/16 × 11
D	Top and bottom shelf facing	4 pcs.	7/8 × 1 × 12
E	Middle shelf facing	4 pcs.	11/16 × 1 × 12
F	Wedge	8 pcs.	1/2 × 13/16 × 3 5/8

3 With a paring chisel and a wooden mallet, define the walls of the mortise.

4 Mark the tusk tenons on the upper and lower shelves using the mortises as guides. Then, cut tenons on the band saw.

GLUE-UP

1 Sand parts before assembly, even though additional sanding will be necessary later.

2 A large number of clamps are required to bring the case together before you can drive the wedges into place through the tusk tenons.

13
BOX WITH RAISED PANELS

Cherry

Raised panels can be created in several different ways. Historically, they were formed using hand planes designed for this specific purpose. In the chapter discussing the Shaker candlebox, a variation of this method (involving a jack plane and a block plane) was used to make the box's sliding lid. Most contemporary cabinetmakers use a table saw or shaper to create raised panels. Typically, these are enclosed in a frame and used as cabinet doors or as doors on kitchen and bathroom cupboards.

The raised panels that appear on the front, back and ends of this box were created on the table saw, but unlike panels used as cabinet and cupboard doors, these are not enclosed in frames nor designed to avoid the problems of cross-grained construction. On this particular box, the raised panels are strictly decorative.

MAKING THE BOX
WITH RAISED PANELS

After the material has been selected and dimensioned, plough grooves on the inside faces of the box's sides and ends to receive the tongues on the edges of the box's top and bottom. Cut dovetails at each of the box's four vertical corners.

Glue the dovetails and assemble the four walls of the box around the top and bottom. At first, this may seem strange because this makes the box a completely sealed enclosure, allowing no access to the space inside. This problem, however, will be solved very quickly.

Because of the placement of the groove near the top of the inside faces of the front, back and ends, the top panel is already raised ⅛″. After the pins and tails at each of the box's vertical corners have been sanded flush, the four vertical panels are raised by cutting a ⁷⁄₁₆″ × ⅛″ pass around all four sides.

You can do this on either the table saw or on a table-mounted router by removing enough material to give the effect of raising the central portion of each of the vertical panels.

Create a lid by cutting a saw kerf through the four walls of the box 1⅞″ from the top.

After installing the hardware (see chapter twenty-seven), cut a shallow mortise around the strike plate, and fasten the ⅛″ thick pull into place with glue and a few brads.

The box is then ready for sanding and finishing.

1 Clamp a strip of wood to the saw fence. This wood will protect the blade when the fence is crowded against it. Then, set the blade at a height of ⁷⁄₁₆″ above the saw table, and bring the fence up to it.

2 The box's four vertical faces are framed by the ⁷⁄₁₆″ × ³⁄₃₂″ saw kerf created when the perimeter of those faces is passed over the blade.

3 Chisels, files and sandpaper are necessary to remove the grain tear-out and burn marks left along the saw kerfs. (This should bring the saw kerf to its finished thickness of ⅛″.)

4 Set the fence 1⅞″ from the blade, and cut off the top, creating the lid.

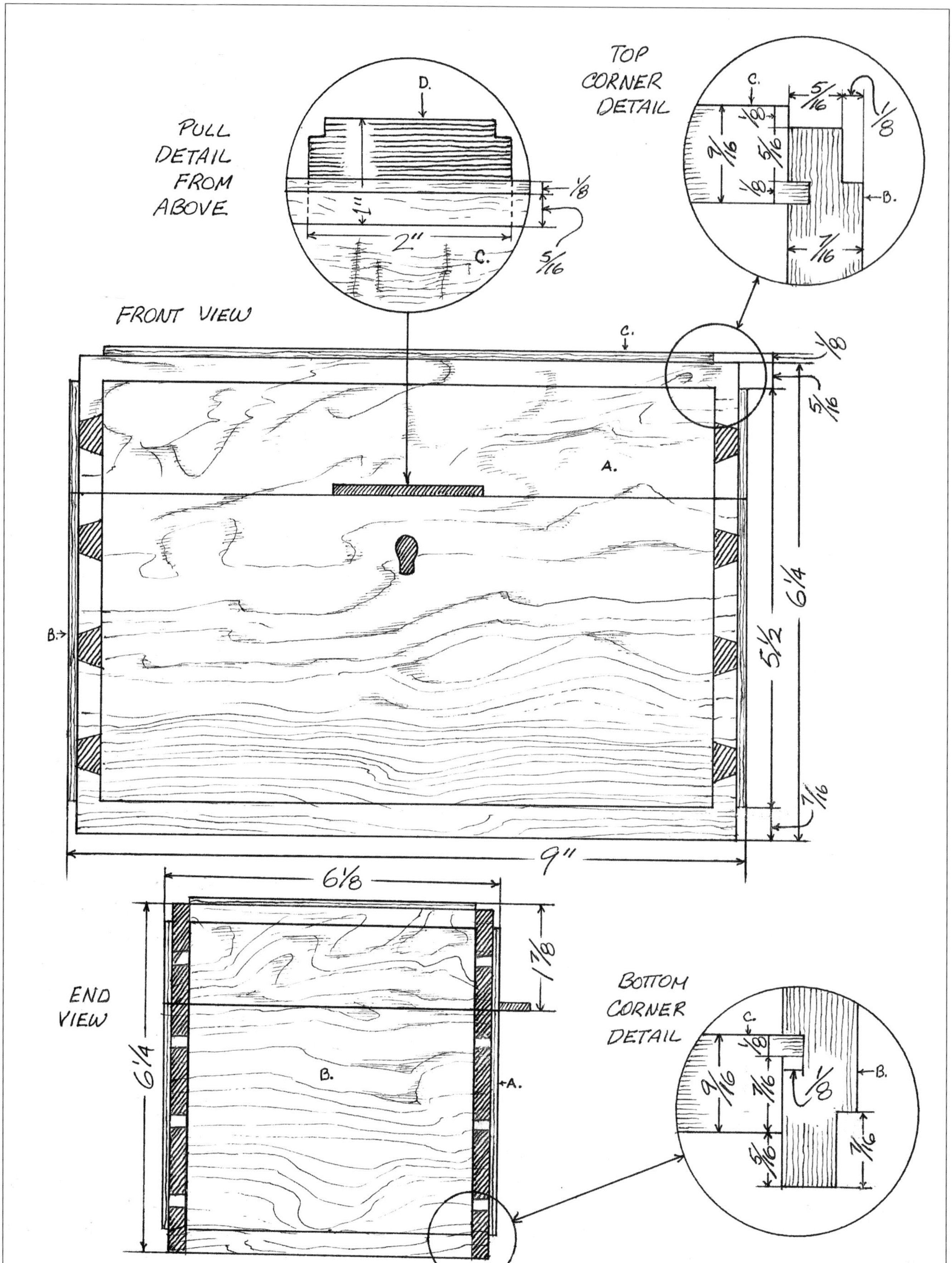
PULL DETAIL FROM ABOVE
D.
1/8
1"
2"
5/16
C.
TOP CORNER DETAIL
C.
5/16
1/8
9/16
1/8
5/16
1/8
B.
7/16
FRONT VIEW
C.
1/8
5/16
A.
B.
6 1/4
5 1/2
7/16
9"
6 1/8
1 7/8
END VIEW
6 1/4
B.
A.
BOTTOM CORNER DETAIL
C.
1/8
9/16
7/16
1/8
B.
5/16
7/16

5 Notice the burn marks left by the saw blade. A blade on which the teeth have set won't burn; however, the hollow-ground planer blade is made without set in order to produce a smoother cut and, as a result, often leaves a burned surface.

BURN REMOVAL

I have read that a hollow-ground planer blade can be persuaded to cut without leaving behind the unsightly, blackened surfaces visible in the above photo. I have read that if the blade is razor sharp, free of pitch, and set perfectly parallel to the rip fence, it is possible to cut without burning.

But I haven't been able to manage it.

I clean the blade frequently, and it is kept sharp, and of course I make an effort to properly set the rip fence, but I always end up with burned surfaces on one or both sides of the cut.

This could be a result of the fact that machine tool maintenance is not a priority in my shop. Although I have the standard array of power tools, I use them no more than necessary and never take pleasure in their operation. They produce too much noise and too much dirt, making the shop a thoroughly unpleasant place to be.

I have, instead, focused on methods for removing these burn makes from cut surfaces.

Those in the above photo are relatively easy to eliminate. Placing the tip of an extremely sharp 1″ butt chisel across the thickness of the blackened wood, I drag the chisel backward (in the direction opposite the bevel) in a scraping motion. Two or three passes removes most of the scorching, in addition to leveling any irregularities left behind by the sawing process. A little work with sandpaper wrapped around a bit of flat scrap then completes the clean-up process.

The scorched areas resulting from the formation of the

MATERIALS LIST			
A	Front and back	2 pcs.	$7/16 \times 6\frac{1}{4} \times 9$
B	End	2 pcs.	$7/16 \times 6\frac{1}{4} \times 6\frac{1}{8}$
C	Bottom and top	2 pcs.	$9/16 \times 5\frac{1}{2} \times 8\frac{3}{8}$
D	Pull	1 pc.	$\frac{1}{8} \times 2 \times 1$
E	Hinges	2 pcs.	$1\frac{1}{2} \times 7/8$
F	Box lock	1 pc.	$1\frac{1}{2} \times 1$

*These are net measurements. A surplus should be added to dovetailed parts to allow joints to be sanded flush.
*Hinges and lock were ordered from Constantine's Hardware.

raised panels on the four sides of this box are a little more difficult. Because the raised panel is immediately adjacent to these flats, they can't be straddled with a chisel. Making the process even more difficult is the fact that the vertical flats on each end of the raised panels run across the grain.

The solution? The only one I know requires patience and a lot of work with a fine-toothed wood file and sandpaper.

I suspect that it would take less time to tune my table saw so that a hollow-ground planer blade wouldn't burn cut surfaces than it does to remove the burn marks afterwards. I suspect that I'm not using my shop time as wisely as I might. But there is a trade-off here. To achieve the overall time savings, I would have resigned myself to several hours of frustrating, knuckle-busting power-tool maintenance, and the truth is that I would rather spend my time scraping and sanding.

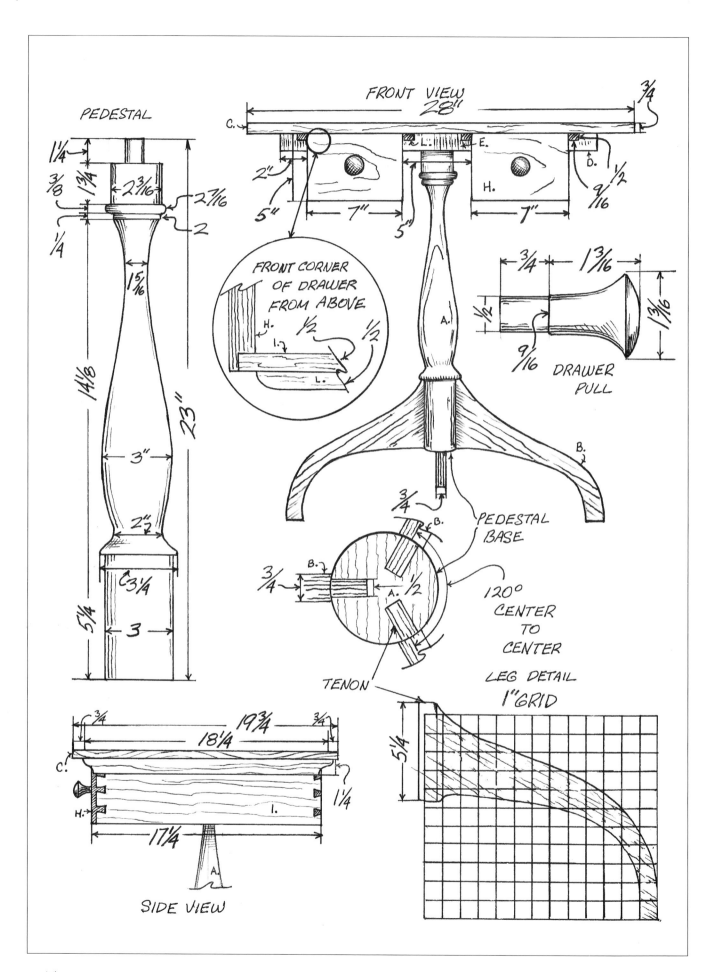

PEDESTAL

FRONT VIEW
28"

FRONT CORNER
OF DRAWER
FROM ABOVE

DRAWER
PULL

PEDESTAL
BASE

120°
CENTER
TO
CENTER

TENON

LEG DETAIL
1" GRID

SIDE VIEW

hole. This process is repeated until I have worked my way to the twelfth hole. Here, I draw another line along the tool rest, marking the centerline of the second leg. Then, counting out twelve more stops on the indexing head, I arrive at the centerline for the third leg.

Although the indexing head simplifies the process of dividing the circumference of the pedestal base into three equal sections, there is an alternative requiring only a compass, a pair of calipers and a rule. First, with the calipers and a rule, determine the diameter of the base. Then, multiply half of that diameter by 1.732. Separate the points of the compass by this distance, and position the stationary leg of the compass at any point on the cylinder's circumference. Make a line along the tool rest at that point. Then, make a second line at the point at which the opposite leg of the compass is farthest from the first line. Then advance the compass so that its stationary leg rests on this second line. Finally, draw a third line along the tool rest where the opposite leg of the compass is farthest from the second line, completing the process of dividing the circumference of this cylinder into three equal sections.

Fit the three legs of this stand into 5¼" long sliding dovetails cut into the base of this pedestal. To this point, I've cut the joints on every pedestal table I've made by hand, and it is inevitably a laborious process. To cut the dovetail mortise, I place the pedestal between 1"-thick blocks of Styrofoam held in place by a towel wrapped in tape, securing the entire, awkward assembly in my vise. This method works but it is slow and a bit clumsy.

The dovetail tenons are even more difficult to cut. I begin these by scoring lines which mark the shoulders on the faces of the ¾"-thick legs. Then, crowding the teeth of a fine-toothed backsaw against the waste side of this line, I cut the shoulders. Complicating this process even further is the fact that the shoulders have to be undercut so that they form a sharp knife-like edge. This is necessary so the shoulders make tight contact with the round base.

Maintaining an accurate alignment along the full 5¼" length of these shoulders is very tricky, but not as tricky as cutting the face of the dovetail. This cut begins on the end grain of the leg and, like the shoulder, was a full 5¼" long. The saw delights in wandering to one side.

After having made several of these stands with hand-cut sliding dovetails, I'm ready to suggest some alternatives. First, if I were to make another with the dovetail joints, I would take the time to build a fixture that would allow the dovetail mortises to be cut with a router while the pedestal is still mounted on the lathe. A reeding or fluting fixture would work nicely for this purpose. The tenons, of

course, could be readily cut on a table-mounted router.

But I really believe that, if I were to make another of these stands, I would drop the dovetail joints and switch to mortise-and-tenon construction. Not only would this be much easier to cut, it would, I think, result in no loss of strength since it would provide an equal amount of glue surface and, at least in this particular application, there is little mechanical advantage to the dovetail joint.

After profiling the legs on the band saw and fitting their tenons into the mortises cut into the pedestal, flatten and smooth the tabletop (see chapter five) and cut to its final length and width. Then, profile the ends of the cleats on the band saw, and cut rabbets for the drawer runners.

Using a backsaw, cut the tenon at the top of the pedestal to its 1" × 1" final size. Cut a matching mortise into the center of the middle cleat. Dry-fit this to the tenon.

At this point, fasten cleats to the bottom of the tabletop using no. 12 wood screws passing through oversized holes (holes that will allow the top to expand and contract in response to seasonal changes in humidity) in the cleats.

Build the drawers with through dovetails at the back and half-blind dovetails at the front. Screw drawer runners to the tops of the drawer sides and fit them to the rabbets in which they will slide. Turn and install pulls. Fasten drawer stops (two blocks of wood screwed to the underside of the top) into place. The piece is ready to finish.

MATERIALS LIST			
Table			
A	Pedestal	1 pc.	3¼ × 23
B	Leg	4 pcs.	¾ × 5¼ × 18
C	Top	1 pc.	¾ × 19¾ × 28
D	Outside cleat	2 pcs.	1¼ × 2 × 18¼
E	Middle cleat	1 pc.	1¼ × 5 × 18¼
F	Drawer stop	2 pcs.	½ × ½ × ¾
G	Screws	various	
Drawers			
H	Front	2 pcs.	¾ × 5 × 7
I	Side	4 pcs.	½ × 5 × 17¼
J	Back	2 pcs.	½ × 5 × 7
K	Bottom	2 pcs.	½ × 4½ × 17
L	Runner	4 pcs.	½ × ½ × 15¾
M	Pull	2 pcs.	1³⁄₁₆ × 1¹⁵⁄₁₆
N	Screws	various	

These are net measurements. A surplus should be added to dovetailed parts to allow them to be sanded flush.

15

WALL BOX

Hard Maple

The original that inspired this piece, an eighteenth-century wall box from New York State, had sides rabbeted and nailed into the front, and a back rabbeted and nailed into the sides. This joinery, although inelegant, permitted the grain in the back to run vertically, which gave a fair amount of strength to the wooden circle from which the original was suspended.

Because dovetail joinery requires horizontal grain on all four sides, my decision to use this joint weakened the wood circle by allowing grain to run out to the right and left. To compensate for this weakness, I grafted in a piece of vertically grained stock behind the wooden circle.

MAKING THE WALL BOX

After the material has been dimensioned, lay out the scroll-work on the back. Once the location of the top circle is established but before the scrollwork is cut out on the band saw, cut a dado across the grain on the back side of this circle. This dado should extend well below the narrow throat on which the top circle is resting. Fit a strip of vertically grained wood into that dado and fasten with ⅜″ no. 4 wood screws. Then, cut out the scrollwork.

After establishing the angle for the two sides, cut the top edge of the front to match. You can do this on the table saw by ripping the piece to width on a blade canted at the proper angle, but I find it quicker to create that angle with a few strokes of a hand plane. Use a bevel gauge to check progress during this operation.

Remember that the angle on the box's front piece is not cut to match the height of the sides at their front most point because the highest point of the angle on the front piece will join the sides ⁷⁄₁₆″ back from the frontmost point. The ⁷⁄₁₆″ measurement allows ⅜″ for the thickness of the dovetail joint, plus a ¹⁄₁₆″ surplus which will be sanded away to make the joint flush.

Cut the dovetails at each of the box's corners. After sanding these flush, give the bottom of the box and the lid shaped edges on a shaper or a table-mounted router. Install the bottom with wood screws passing through over-sized holes in the bottom. These holes are oversized to allow the part to expand and contract in response to seasonal changes in humidity.

The narrow top, to which the lid will be hinged, is the next consideration. Form the angled front edge, which will abut the angled back edge of the lid, with a hand plane. Then fasten it to the case with several screws passing through the back of the box. Although I felt it unnecessary because of the top's narrow width, this part might be more securely fastened by installing some short glue blocks underneath the joint between the top and the sides of the case.

Using a hand plane, fit the back edge of the lid to the angle already established on the front edge of the box's top. Do this gradually so that it can be fit against the front edge of the top without gapping at the ends.

Next, install the hinges. The pair shown in the photo are Brainerd antique brass hinges from which the tails on the upper leaves have been cut to allow those upper leaves to fit on the narrow width of the top of the box.

Remove the hinges and give the box a final sanding and several coats of finish.

1 Butt this wide, straight edge up to the fence on the radial arm saw and cut the dado before the back is profiled.

2 Hold the reinforcing strip in place with four ⅜″ no. 4 wood screws. After installing it, cut the scrollwork.

3 Drill oversized screw holes through the bottom.

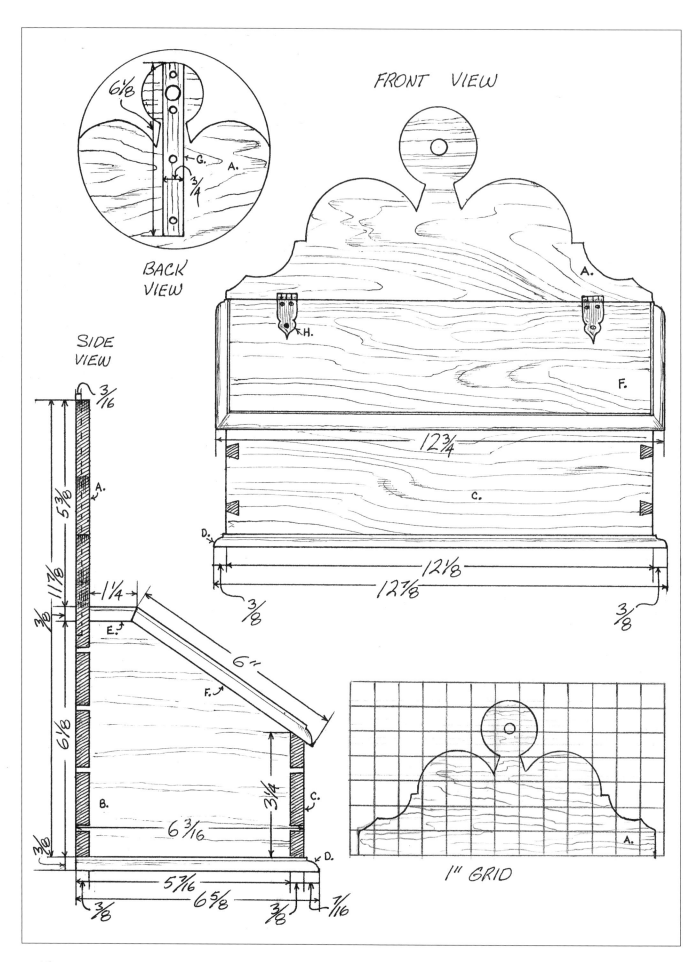

BACK
VIEW

FRONT VIEW

SIDE
VIEW

1" GRID

MAKING THE WALL BOX <small>(CONTINUED)</small>

4 Hold the bottom in place with masking tape while driving the screws up into the box's frame.

5 With the box held upside down in a vise, fasten the bottom.

6 Check frequently to ensure that the top and the lid will come together without gaps.

MATERIALS LIST			
A	Back	1 pc.	$\frac{3}{8} \times 11\frac{7}{8} \times 12\frac{1}{8}$
B	Side	2 pcs.	$\frac{3}{8} \times 6\frac{1}{8} \times 6\frac{3}{16}$
C	Front	1 pc.	$\frac{3}{8} \times 3\frac{1}{4} \times 12\frac{1}{8}$
D	Bottom	1 pc.	$\frac{3}{8} \times 6\frac{5}{8} \times 12\frac{7}{8}$
E	Top	1 pc.	$\frac{3}{8} \times 1\frac{1}{4} \times 12\frac{3}{4}$
F	Lid	1 pc.	$\frac{3}{8} \times 6 \times 12\frac{3}{4}$
G	Reinforcing strip	1 pc.	$\frac{3}{16} \times \frac{3}{4} \times 6\frac{1}{8}$
H	Hinge	2 pc.	$3\frac{1}{4} \times \frac{1}{2}$
I	Screws	14 pcs.	$\frac{3}{4}''$ no. 6

These are net measurements. A surplus should be added to dovetailed parts to allow them to be sanded flush.

16

CHIPPENDALE MIRROR

Cherry, Walnut

Although shaper cutters and router bits come in a bewildering array of shapes and sizes, the exact configuration required for a particular project isn't always available. But often, through some imaginative blending of manufactured shapes (sometimes mixed with a little handwork), the woodworker can create the necessary forms.

The moulding which frames the glass on this Chippendale mirror was produced through the use of two three-winged shaper cutters and a little rabbet work on the tablesaw.

DESIGNED BY

JIM PIERCE

MAKING THE CHIPPENDALE MIRROR

Although not a reproduction of any specific eighteenth-century original, this mirror does evoke a number of Chippendale designs.

Begin construction with the scrollwork background. After the pieces have been band sawn and sanded, assemble them with butt joints and hold in place with a pair of cleats which are glued and screwed across the back of the scrollwork. At that time, take measurements for the large moulding which lifts and presents the glass.

Working with these measurements and the available shaper cutters and router bits, you can determine the moulding's profile. After the stock has been run, miter the four pieces of the moulded frame to length and screw into place. Complete finishing before installing the mirror to avoid sullying its surface. Tack four wood strips to the back, inside face of the moulding, to hold it in place.

This close-up shows how the scrollwork, tack strip and cleat are assembled.

MATERIALS LIST			
A	Vertical scrollwork	2 pcs.	½ × 2¼ × 24¼
B	Top scrollwork	1 pc.	½ × 6⅞ × 14⅛
C	Bottom scrollwork	1 pc.	½ × 4¾ × 14⅛
D	Horizontal moulding	2 pcs.	1¼ × 1¼ × 14⅞
E	Vertical moulding	2 pcs.	1¼ × 1¼ × 19½
F	Cleat	2 pcs.	⁵⁄₁₆ × 1½ × 16⅛
G	Vertical tack strip	2 pcs.	¼ × ½ × 17⁹⁄₁₆
H	Horizontal tack strip	2 pcs.	¼ × ½ × 12⅞
I	Mirror back	1 pc.	⅛ × 12⅞ × 17⁹⁄₁₆
J	Mirror	1 pc.	Exact measurements should be taken after the frame has been constructed.

CHIPPENDALE

What are the characteristics of Chippendale furniture?

In the strictest sense, the only furniture that can be identified as Chippendale is that to which Thomas Chippendale, the English carver and designer actually applied his tools. But there are few such pieces and many that are commonly (and usefully) referred to as Chippendale.

Another approach reserves the Chippendale name for those pieces that are exact representations of his published drawings. But this, too, is very limiting, particularly when discussing furniture made in North America. While there are a handful of American-made pieces which accurately represent specific Chippendale designs, the overwhelming majority of American-made Chippendale furniture does not—for some very good reasons.

Thomas Chippendale, George Hepplewhite and Thomas Sheraton—the English designers whose seminal books inspired much American period furniture—all designed for a different market than that served by most American craftsmen of the day. Many of the English designs were intended for placement in grand English homes and included, therefore, elaborate ornamentation that was inappropriate for less palatial American settings (and perhaps for less effete American sensibilities).

This doesn't mean that discriminating American buyers weren't concerned about the appearance of their furniture. Clearly they were, but what those buyers wanted was furniture that not only looked good but was also, and most importantly, useful. They wanted storage, serving surfaces, beds. In short, they wanted furniture in which function and form were more fully integrated.

To address this desire on the part of their customers, American designers/craftsmen reinterpreted the forms presented in the books of the English designers, restraining the decorative excesses of the originals, focusing on the usefulness of their furniture in the homes of their customers.

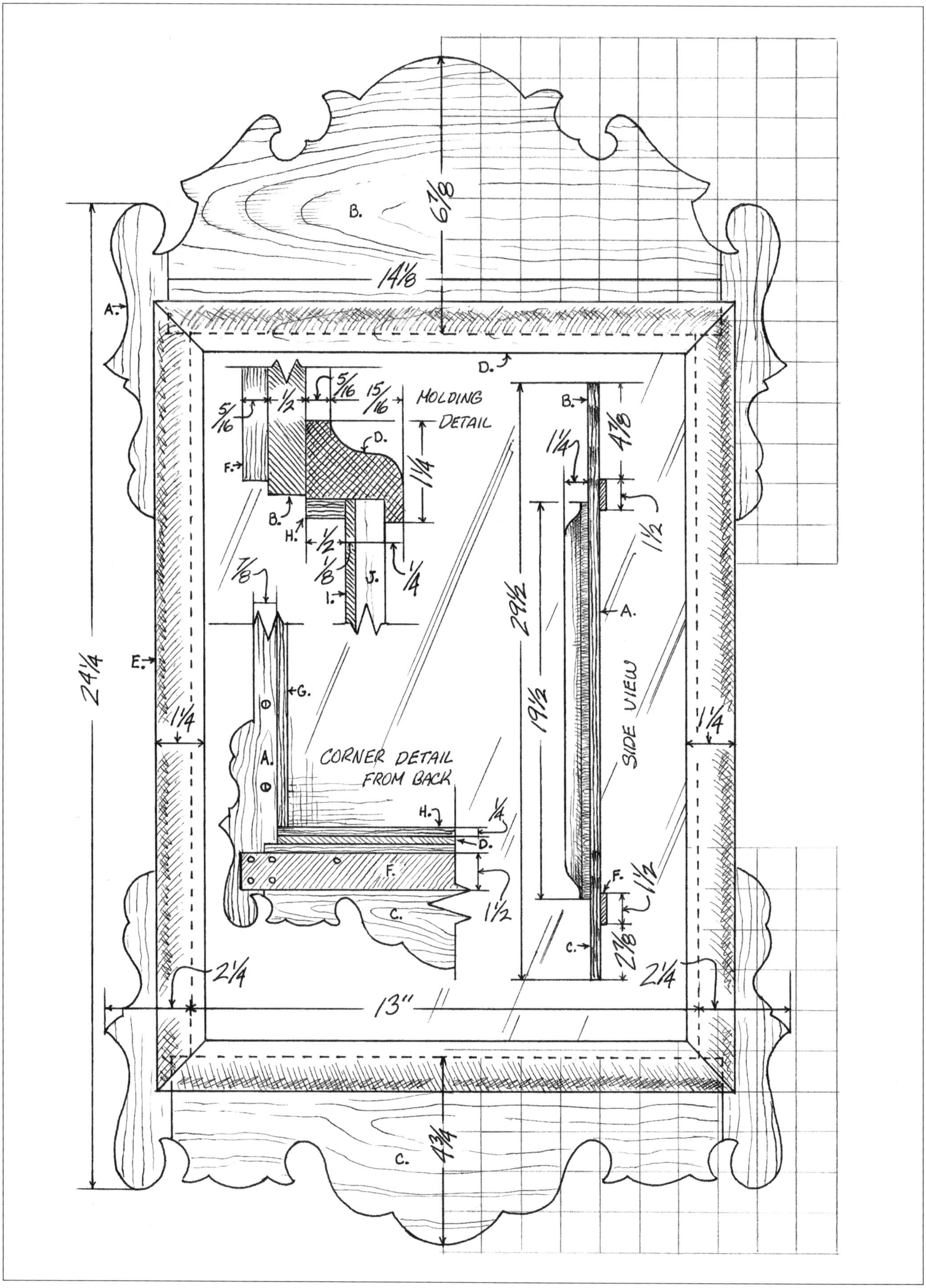
B.
6 7/8
14 1/8
A.
D.
MOLDING DETAIL
5/16
1/2
5/16
15/16
D.
1 1/4
F.
B.
H.
1/2
1/8
1/4
J.
I.
7/8
G.
E.
24 1/4
1 1/4
A.
CORNER DETAIL FROM BACK
H.
1/4
D.
F.
1 1/2
C.
2 1/4
13"
B.
4 7/8
1 1/4
1/2
29 1/2
19 1/2
SIDE VIEW
A.
F.
1 1/2
C.
2 7/8
2 1/4
C.
4 3/4

This makes stylistic attribution a slippery business. Even though almost all high-style American furniture of the late eighteenth and early nineteenth centuries exhibits characteristics of Chippendale, Hepplewhite and Sheraton designs, very little actually represents any specific published drawings. Further complicating the business of stylistic attribution is the fact that many pieces exhibit characteristics of more than one style. A sideboard might have a spade foot (a Hepplewhite signature) and a gallery of turned spindles (associated with Sheraton's designs). A chair might have a balloon back and solid splat (Queen Anne) and ball-and-claw feet (Chippendale).

In the hands of a skilled craftsman, such blending is unimportant. A well-designed chair is a well-designed chair whatever the origins of its iconography.

But for the student of furniture, it can be useful to look at this matter of stylistic attribution—not to fasten a particular label on a particular piece but in order to reflect on the American designer/craftsman's handling of the forms and motifs with which he worked.

With that in mind, I put together the following chart:

STYLE CHARACTERISTICS

This chart is not intended to list all the elements of any of these styles. It is meant only to illustrate ways in which one style might be differentiated from another.

	CHIPPENDALE	HEPPLEWHITE	SHERATON	EMPIRE
form	syma curve	geometrical curvilinear	geometrical rectilinear delicate	massive
ornament	carving scrollwork	stringing veneering inlay	turning bandings carving reeding	carving veneering ormolu
motif	cabriole leg ball-and-claw foot	spade foot tapered legs	turned and tapered legs	animal feet animal heads

17
HEPPLEWHITE-STYLE END TABLE

Cherry, Birch, White Pine

The late Carlyle Lynch did a number of beautifully rendered drawings of period furniture, several of which appeared on the pages of *Fine Woodworking*. In our living room, there is a three-quarter-size Queen Anne highboy built from one of his drawings and a Hepplewhite-style huntboard based on another serves as a TV stand.

As companion pieces to the huntboard, I built a pair of end tables, the legs of which, although more delicate, have tapers similar to those on the Lynch-drawn huntboard.

MAKING THE HEPPLEWHITE-STYLE END TABLE

Select, plane, joint and edge-glue material for the top.

Set aside the top panel, and prepare the legs. First, dimension the leg stock to $^{15}/_{16}" \times {}^{15}/_{16}"$. Then mark and cut the mortises for the apron parts and the drawer rails, and draw the taper on the leg stock with a pencil.

On the face of the leg that will be seen from the side of the table, the legs taper from $^{15}/_{16}"$ at the lower limit of the apron to $\frac{1}{2}"$ at the floor. On the face of the legs that will be seen from the ends of the table, the legs taper from $^{15}/_{16}"$ to $\frac{3}{8}"$.

Cut the tapers on the band saw; clamp the leg in a vise so that saw marks can be removed with a hand plane.

Cut out and tenon apron parts and drawer rails. Fit these tenons into the leg mortises which are placed so that the outside faces of the apron parts are recessed $\frac{1}{8}"$ from the outside faces of the legs. Set the drawer rails, on the other hand, so that their outside faces are flush with the outside faces of the legs. Then, glue-up the frame—consisting of the apron parts, the drawer rails and the legs.

Remove the tabletop from the clamps, and surface it with hand planes and sandpaper, a process discussed in chapter five.

Next, cut the grooves for the inlay. You could make these with a router, but I cut the grooves on this top on a table saw fit with a hollow-ground planer blade. This blade is made without set and with a thin-ground rim. As a result, it leaves a $^{3}/_{32}"$ saw kerf with sharp, clean edges.

Rip out the birch inlay itself using the same planer blade passing through a combination wood fence and throat that is clamped to the saw's steel fence. Glue the inlay into its grooves; plane and sand flat.

Because the top will expand and contract across its width in response to seasonal changes in humidity, fasten it to

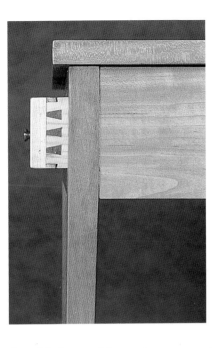

This close-up of the drawer side shows the cock bead inlay around the drawer.

the table frame with wood screws passing through oversized holes in the kicker strips. (The kicker strips are the two cleats above the drawer sides that keep the front of the drawer from dropping as the drawer is opened.) The oversized holes in the kicker strips will allow wood movement without splitting the top.

Drawer construction is standard. Use through dovetails at the back of the drawer and half-blind dovetails at the front. (Both joints are discussed in chapter twenty-five.)

Rip strips for the $^{3}/_{32}"$ cock bead (thin, mitered strips framing the drawer front) from $\frac{7}{8}"$ birch stock. Next, plane them. To round the front edge of the cock bead, clamp the strips of $^{3}/_{32}"$ planed stock in a vise between thicker, wider boards so that approximately $\frac{1}{4}"$ sits above the clamping boards along the full length of the strips. Then with a block plane, remove enough material to round the front edges of the strips.

Next cut rabbets for the cock bead. This operation is done on the table saw, again using a hollow-ground planer blade. The blade is set to a height $\frac{1}{8}"$ less than the width of the cock bead ($\frac{5}{8}"$). Then, with the blade crowded against a wood fence, take a single pass from the top, bottom and both ends of the drawer which stands on its front end.

This cuts a rabbet $^{3}/_{32}"$ wide which is equal to the thickness of the cock bead. With brads and glue, fasten the mitered cock bead to the drawer front so that its rounded edge stands $\frac{1}{8}"$ proud of the face of the drawer front.

After installing the drawer runners and stops, the table is ready for finishing and hardware.

Shown here is the combination fence and throat I use for ripping inlay and cock bead.

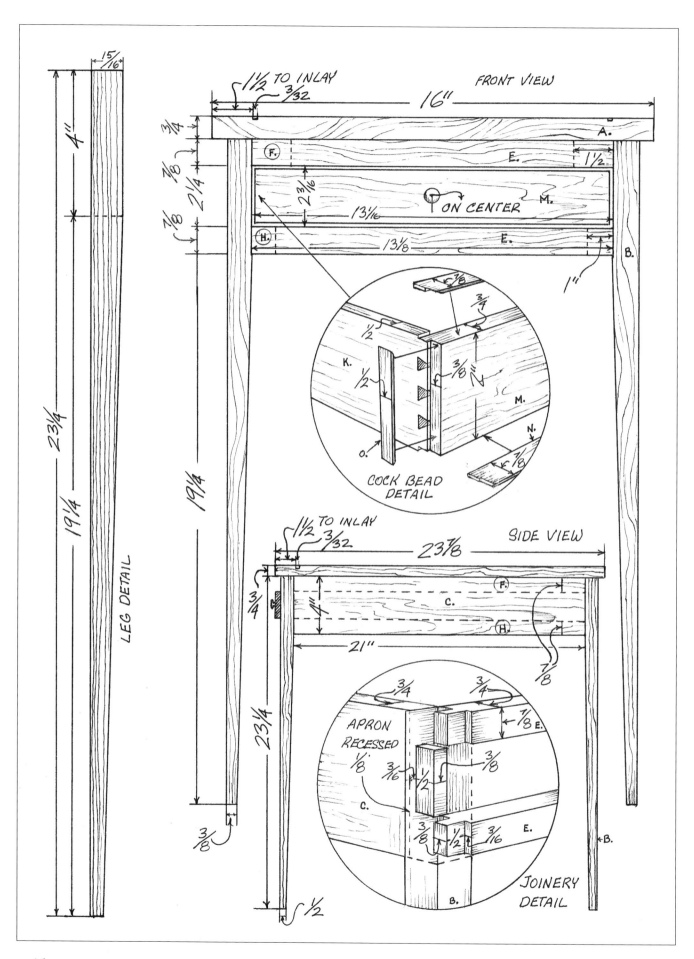

15/16

4"

1½ TO INLAY
3/32
FRONT VIEW
16"
A.

3/4
F.
E.
1½

7/8
2 3/16
13/16
ON CENTER
M.

7/8
2¼
H.
13⅛
E.
B.

1"

23¾

19¼

19¼

½
1/2
K.
1/2
3/4
3/8
M.
N.
7/8
O.

COCK BEAD
DETAIL

1½ TO INLAY
3/32
SIDE VIEW
23⅞
F.

3/4
3/4
4"
C.
H.
7/8

21"

APRON
RECESSED
1/8
3/4
3/4
7/8 E.
3/16
1/2
3/8
C.
3/8
1/2
3/16
E.
B.

23¾

3/8

½

B.

JOINERY
DETAIL

LEG DETAIL

FURNITURE DESIGN

Almost 150 pages of Thomas Sheraton's *The Cabinet-Maker and Upholsterer's Drawing Book*, a collection of some of the most influential furniture designs ever published, is focused on geometry, including almost thirty pages on the five classical orders of proportion taken from the five types of Roman columns: Tuscan, Doric, Ionic, Composite and Corinthian.

This lengthy exposition on the subjects of geometry and proportion highlights the importance of formal design education to the makers of period originals. This is an education that many modern designers/craftsmen lack. Some contemporary woodworkers, guided by enormous natural talent, seem unhindered by this absence. Others, however, lacking both the talent and the education, are creating furniture which, while well-crafted, is often clumsy in appearance.

Although not guided by either an enormous natural talent or by a classical design education, I've found that, in order to do business, it has been necessary for me to design work to suit my customer's needs. What follows is a list of commonsense principles I've found useful:

1. ***Steal from the past.*** Wood furniture has a history that stretches back at least five thousand years, and throughout that span designers and craftsmen have struggled with the same question confronting woodworkers today: How can chairs, beds, tables and chests be designed so that they are both beautiful and useful?

Clearly, no single answer to this question is perfect. If it were, we would have only one style of bed, chair or table. But many of the hard-won solutions created by our predecessors are worthy of study and emulation.

2. ***Take chances.*** Particularly at the pencil and paper stage, the most bizarre ideas deserve consideration because, although they may never be translated whole into actual pieces of furniture, a careful examination may reveal things that can be incorporated into more traditional forms.

3. ***Consider aesthetics and joinery simultaneously.*** Often, designs that look spectacular on paper simply can't be created from wood, a natural material with a whole range of characteristics that must be considered each time one wood part is joined to another.

4. ***Develop graceful lines.*** When I designed the two-drawer sewing stand (after several Shaker originals), I worked to create a curve in the legs that would move smoothly into the curves of the pedestal. I hoped this

would lift the eye to the tabletop and drawers, as well as produce a line that was inherently satisfying to contemplate.

5. ***Repeat motifs.*** Repetition of a shape, pattern or color can give a piece both rhythm and unity. On the six-drawer chest, for example, the cone shape of the pulls is repeated six times across the front of the drawers, adding visual rhythm in much the same way that a repeated drumbeat can add auditory rhythm to a piece of music. Also, that tapered cone shape is repeated in the four legs that support the chest, assuring the viewer that all these parts belong to the same piece.

6. ***Incorporate exposed joinery.*** A set of dovetails marching across the corner of a piece not only adds rhythm (see photo on page 26), it also adds an appealing

MATERIALS LIST

Table

A	Top	1 pc.	$\frac{3}{4} \times 16 \times 23\frac{7}{8}$
B	Leg	4 pcs.	$1\frac{5}{16} \times 1\frac{5}{16} \times 23\frac{1}{4}$
C	Apron side	2 pcs.	$\frac{3}{4} \times 4 \times 22^{1}$
D	Apron end	1 pc.	$\frac{3}{4} \times 4 \times 14\frac{1}{8}^{1}$
E	Drawer rail	2 pcs.	$\frac{7}{8} \times \frac{3}{4} \times 14\frac{1}{8}^{1}$
F	Kicker strip	2 pcs.	$\frac{7}{8} \times 1\frac{1}{2} \times 21$
G	Cleat	1 pc.	$\frac{7}{8} \times 1\frac{1}{2} \times 10$
H	Drawer runner	2 pcs.	$\frac{7}{8} \times 1 \times 21$
I	Inlay		$\frac{3}{32} \times \frac{3}{32} \times 7$ linear feet

Drawer

J	Bottom	1 pc.	$\frac{1}{2} \times 12\frac{5}{8} \times 15\frac{3}{4}$
K	Side	2 pcs.	$\frac{1}{2} \times 2\frac{3}{16} \times 16\frac{1}{8}$
L	End	1 pc.	$\frac{1}{2} \times 1\frac{5}{8} \times 13\frac{1}{16}$
M	Front	1 pc.	$\frac{3}{4} \times 2\frac{3}{16} \times 13\frac{1}{16}$
N	Horizontal cock bead	2 pcs.	$\frac{3}{32} \times \frac{7}{8} \times 13\frac{1}{16}$
O	Vertical cock bead	2 pcs.	$\frac{3}{32} \times \frac{1}{2} \times 2\frac{3}{16}$
P	Pull	1 pc.	$\frac{1}{2} \times \frac{1}{2}$

¹*Includes ½" tenon on each end.*
*Net measurements are given. A surplus should be added to the lengths of dovetailed parts to allow them to be sanded flush.
*Drawer height and width are ¹⁄₁₆" less than the height and width of drawer opening. This allows ¹⁄₃₂" of clearance on all four sides.
*The pull was ordered from Constantine's Hardware.

visual detail, which arrests the eye, satisfying its hunger for interesting shapes and patterns.

7. ***Adapt stock thickness to the scale of the piece.*** Smaller, more delicate pieces require stock dimensioned to a greater thinness. A plate rack that is elegant when built from ⅜″ material is brutish and clumsy when built from ⅞″ stock.

8. ***Use beautiful materials.*** Yes, hardwood—particularly figured hardwood—is expensive, but the simplest pieces (the Shaker document chest, for example) are enormously appealing when built with beautiful material.

9. ***Use contrasting materials.*** A desk made entirely of walnut heartwood can be very attractive. But imagine that same desk with curly maple drawer fronts or with streaks of walnut sapwood showing like jagged lightning across the top.

10. ***Recognize that design is as much an evolutionary process as a revolutionary process.*** Rather than focusing on sweeping changes that might be made to the form of a chair, bed or chest, a designer might be better served by focusing on small, incremental changes which, over time, might add up to something significant.

DESIGN EVOLUTION

These photos illustrate the evolutionary development of an arm shape I've used on many Shaker-style chairs.

1 The first photo shows one of my earliest attempts to elaborate on the cookie-cutter shapes of the Shaker original.

2 The second shows an arm that's been widened and given a more distinct form.

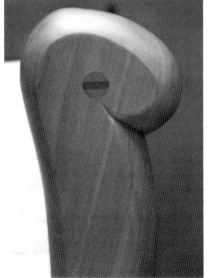

3 The last two photos show details of a more recent chair.

4 The incised curve on the top of the arm now reaches to the wedged through tenon at the top of the chair's front post, a shape that recurs on the chair's slat.

18

TWO-DRAWER CHEST

Curly Maple, Cherry, Beech, Poplar

The original on which this chest is based, described by John Kassay in *The Book of Shaker Furniture*, was used in the Shaker community at Hancock, Massachusetts. Kassay describes the lower drawer as having been used for "tools and larger items." He is less specific about the use to which the upper drawer was put, noting only that it was "divided into fifteen small sections."

Although the photo in Kassay's book doesn't show the interior of the upper drawer, in all likelihood the technique by which that interior was compartmentalized is the same as that used in making the reproduction shown here, a technique known as *egg crating*.

DESIGNED BY
JIM PIERCE

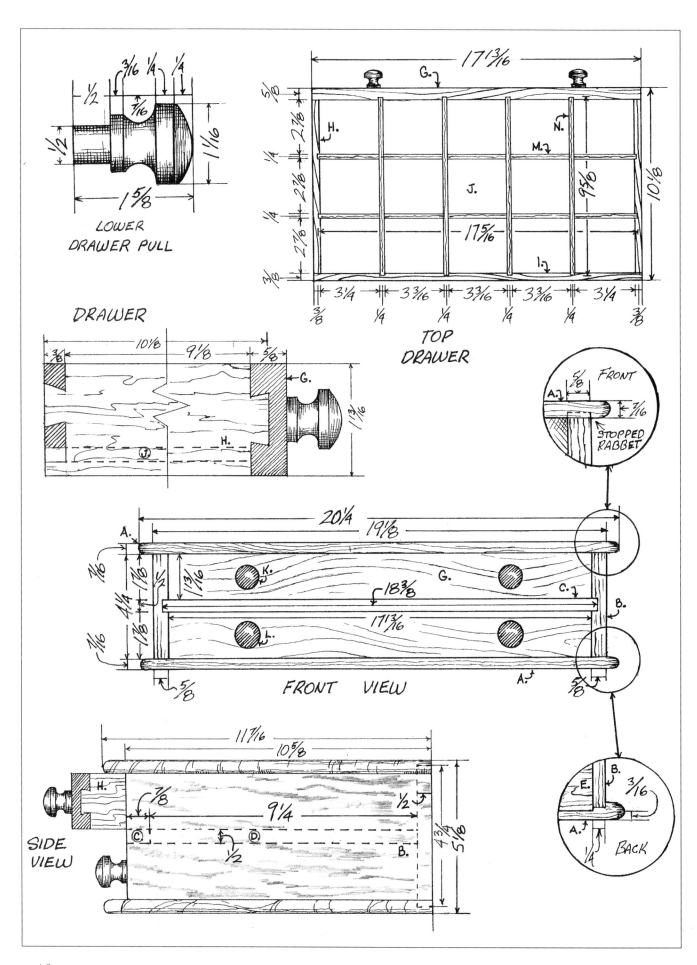

MAKING THE TWO-DRAWER CHEST

After the material has been dimensioned, cut the joints for the case. First, cut the ⅛″ × ⅝″ stopped dadoes on the top and bottom that will receive the case sides. (See chapter five for information about cutting a stopped joint on the table saw.) Then cut the ⁵⁄₁₆″ × ½″ rabbet along the back inside edges of the case sides and a ¼″ × ½″ rabbet along the back inside edges of the top and bottom. Although the side rabbets run the length of the stock, the rabbets on the top and bottom are stopped on both ends. (Chapter five discusses a method for making stopped grooves and rabbets on the table saw.) Finally, cut the dadoes that will receive the dust panel and the drawer rail. Assemble the case with glue and screws. Fit plugs into the countersunk screw holes in the case's top.

Build the drawers next. The bottom drawer is a simple box, the parts of which are joined together with a single fat dovetail at each corner, through at the back, half-blind at the front (see chapter twenty-five). The upper drawer, compartmentalized by egg crating, is a little more complex.

After the egg crate stock has been dimensioned, dado the interior faces of the drawer sides, front and back to receive the ends of the crating material. Lay out and cut the half-slots that will join the pieces of the crating material. For this particular drawer, the slots were cut on the bottom half of the short lengths and the top half of the long lengths.

MATERIALS LIST			
Case			
A	Top and bottom	1 pc.	⁷⁄₁₆ × 11⁷⁄₁₆ × 20¼
B	Side	2 pcs.	⅝ × 4½ × 10⅝
C	Drawer rail	1 pc.	½ × ⅞ × 18⅜
D	Dust panel	1 pc.	½ × 9¼ × 18⅜
E	Back	1 pc.	½ × 5 × 18⅜
F	Plug	8 pcs.	⅜ × ¼
Drawers			
G	Front	2 pcs.	⅝ × 1¹³⁄₁₆ × 17¹³⁄₁₆
H	Side	4 pcs.	⅜ × 1¹³⁄₁₆ × 10⅛
I	Back	2 pcs.	⅜ × 1⁷⁄₁₆ × 17¾
J	Bottom	2 pcs.	¼ × 9¾ × 17¼
K	Upper pull	2 pcs.	1 × 1½
L	Lower pull	2 pcs.	1¹⁄₁₆ × 1⅝
Egg crating			
M	Long	2 pcs.	¼ × 1³⁄₁₆ × 17⁵⁄₁₆
N	Short	4 pcs.	¼ × 1¹³⁄₁₆ × 9⅝
Hardware			
O	Screws	various	

These are net measurements. A surplus should be added to dovetailed parts to allow them to be sanded flush.

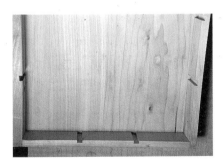

1 Prior to the drawer's assembly, cut dadoes on the inside faces of the drawer front, back and sides.

2 The egg crate components are held together with half-slots.

3 The chest's partially open drawers are shown here from above. Note the shape of the drawer pull.

19

DRYING RACK

White Ash, Walnut

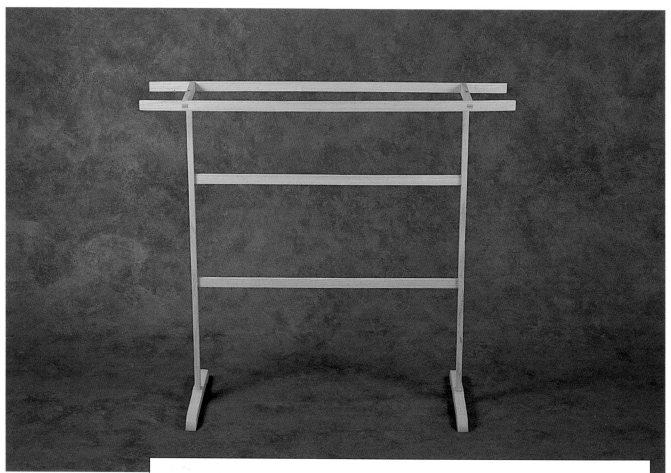

Minimalism is one of the distinguishing characteristics of fine Shaker furniture and woodenware. Over a period of years, beginning in 1800 with rough, country models, the Shakers refined their work, continually paring away thickness, width, ornamentation, even joinery. What resulted, in the middle of the nineteenth century, was a style of furniture in which all but the essential had been stripped away.

This drying rack, taken from John Kassay's *The Book of Shaker Furniture*, is one example. It contains no excess material, it has no tricky forms to shape, and the joinery has been reduced to its simplest terms.

But the simplicity is deceptive. In order for its few parts to come together correctly, so that its right angles are truly 90°, great care must be taken with the cutting and fitting of all twelve through tenons because, with so little joinery, every error in that joinery is magnified.

MAKING THE DRYING RACK

After milling the stock to the required thicknesses, widths and lengths, cut the feet with a band saw.

Form tenons on both ends of the posts and crossbars. This can be done by hand, using a tenon saw, or on a table saw fit with a stack of dado cutters.

Lay out and cut the twelve through mortises. Precision is essential with these tiny joints as the slightest error will multiply over the lengths of the posts, arms and crossbars. When test-fitting these tenons into their mortises, it's important to use a framing square (or other long-armed square) to make frequent checks of all right angles.

Notches for the walnut wedges should be no wider than the kerf of a fine-toothed backsaw. After cutting these notches, dry-assemble the rack. Check angles and joints. Then, knock apart the rack, glue the joints, and drive the tiny walnut wedges into their notches.

After the glue has cured, saw off protruding wedges, pare tenons, and give the piece a final sanding.

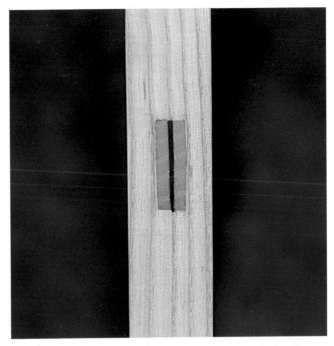

Walnut wedges contrast with the ash through tenon and end grain.

FITTING MATERIAL TO TASK

All woods are not created equal. Among our American hardwoods, some—like cherry and walnut—display striking color. Others—such as oaks, ashes and hickories—have enormous resistance to breaking. Still others—like hard maple—can be turned or carved very finely without detail crumbling away as it might with a coarser wood.

Traditionally, furniture was designed to take advantage of the different characteristics of the different species. The selection of species for the various parts of the Windsor chair illustrates this point. Windsor seats, which must be shaped to conform to the human bottom with hand tools—adzes, inshaves, travishers—were typically made of pine or poplar: softwoods relatively easy to manipulate. The legs were often turned from hard maple which, despite its nondescript color, possesses enormous strength and turns very nicely. Back spindles were usually shaved from white oak which, even when reduced to a tiny diameter, retains great resistance to breaking. This principle of matching material to task was also applied to casework. Primary woods (those used to fashion visible parts) were chosen for the beauty of their color and figure. Imported mahogany, walnut, cherry and figured maples were the traditional choices for this application. Secondary woods (those used to fashion interior components such as drawer parts) were selected for availability, the ease with which they could be worked. For this use, pine and poplar were common choices.

In general, eighteenth- and nineteenth-century woodwork reflected an intimate knowledge of the different qualities of different species of wood.

In an attempt to fit my material to my task, I chose ash for this drying rack because, of all the woods available in my shop, it offered the greatest strength when planed so thinly. This said, I should also point out that the original on which this rack is based was, inexplicably, built of pine.

1 The Shakers delighted in doing much with little. In this single length of ash, there is more than enough material to build two of the Shaker-designed drying racks.

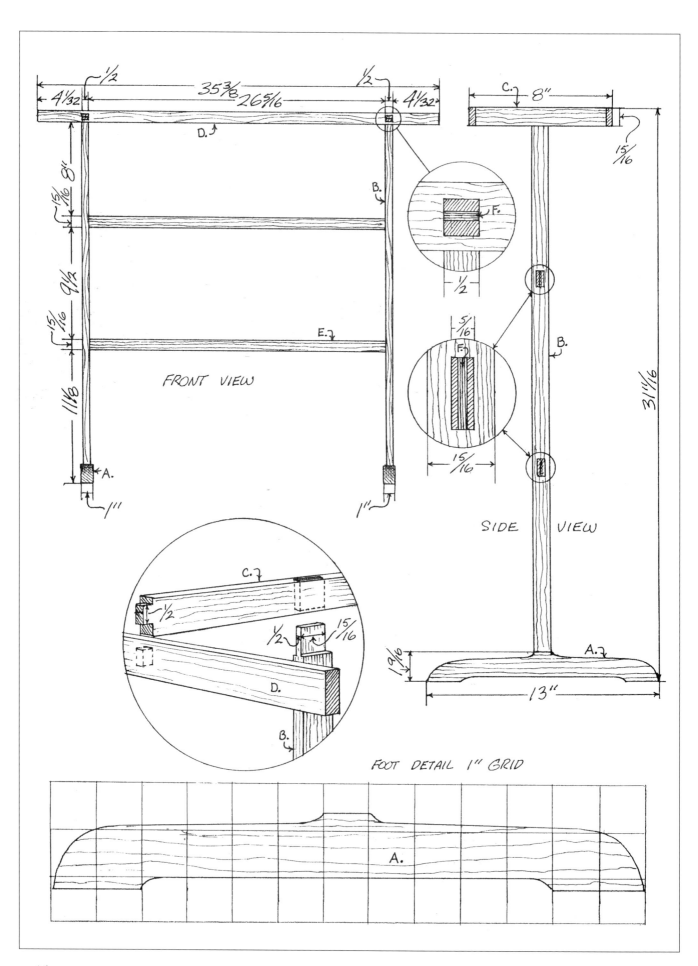

1/2

35 3/8
26 5/16

1/2

4 1/32
4 1/32

D.

8"

C.
8"

15/16

B.

F.

8"

15/16

1/2

9 1/2

15/16

5/16

F.

E.

FRONT VIEW

B.

31 11/16

15/16

1 1/8

15/16

A.

1"

1"

A.

C.

1/2

1/2

15/16

D.

SIDE VIEW

A.

1 9/16

13"

B.

FOOT DETAIL 1" GRID

A.

2 Tenons can be cut on the table saw with a stack of dado cutters.

3 After the parts have been dimensioned, shaped and tenoned, lay out and cut mortises.

MATERIALS LIST			
A	Feet	2 pcs.	$1 \times 1^{9}/_{16} \times 13$
B	Post	2 pcs.	$^{1}/_{2} \times {}^{15}/_{16} \times 31^{7}/_{16}$
C	Crossbar	2 pcs.	$^{1}/_{2} \times {}^{15}/_{16} \times 8$
D	Arm	2 pcs.	$^{5}/_{16} \times {}^{15}/_{16} \times 35^{3}/_{8}$
E	Post brace	2 pcs.	$^{5}/_{16} \times {}^{15}/_{16} \times 27^{5}/_{16}$
F	Wedges	8 pcs.	$^{1}/_{8} \times$ various widths

These are net measurements. Surplus should be added to the lengths to allow through tenons to be sanded flush.

20

SIX-DRAWER CHEST

Curly Maple, Walnut

I started this piece with the intention of making a fairly accurate reproduction of a Shaker apothecary chest; however, I soon found myself making changes from the original in order to accommodate several material and joinery considerations.

First, the drawers on the Shaker piece were assembled using a machine-cut scalloped dovetail joint—one I couldn't reproduce in my shop. Conventional dovetails were the obvious choice, but the half-blind dovetail (used for drawer fronts) requires a fair amount of time, and with six tiny drawers, I searched for alternatives, settling finally on a single through dovetail at each corner of each drawer. Since this joint makes the end grain of the drawer sides visible from the front, I used contrasting woods in order to make those fat dovetails a more emphatic component of the chest's design.

Since the piece seemed to be taking on a contemporary rather than a Shaker look, I decided then to avoid symmetry in drawer placement and to lift the whole case on four tapered cones turned from drawer-front scrap, cones that, to my eye, evoked the legs on a lot of kitschy 1950s furniture.

MAKING THE SIX-DRAWER CHEST

After the stock for the top, bottom and ends of the case has been thicknessed, ripped to width, and cut to length, each must be given a ¼″ × ⁵⁄₁₆″ rabbet that will later receive the back panel. At this time, cut the through dovetails at each corner. The rabbet complicates this process, but there are a couple of easy choices you can make here: (1) miter the material that will house the rabbet, or (2) use a lap joint in which the rabbets on the case's top and bottom simply lap the rabbets on the ends.

After fitting the dovetails, lay out and cut the dadoes for the partitions between drawers. Then glue-up the case.

After the glue on the dovetails has cured, slide the partitions into place with a bit of glue spread in the dadoes. Drive brads through the top, sides and bottom of the case to help hold these partitions.

Fit the tenons at the top of each leg into mortises drilled into the bottom of the case, and affix the back panel in its rabbet using ½″ no. 6 wood screws passing through oversized holes (to allow for wood movement as the panel expands and contracts in response to seasonal changes in humidity) in the panel.

Except for the big, fat dovetail at each corner, drawer construction is conventional. Plough a ¼″ × ¼″ groove on each drawer side and on the back of the front. These will receive the ¼″-thick drawer bottom. The back of the drawer is not as high as the sides; it extends down only as far as

Partially open drawers reveal the fat dovetails.

the top of the drawer bottom. Nail through the drawer bottom, up into this drawer back.

For a larger, weight-carrying drawer, the single dovetail at each corner would be a poor choice, but for such a tiny drawer, one that will never carry more than a few ounces of load, the single dovetail provides a joint offering a fair amount of mechanical resistance to forward pull and a fair amount of glue surface.

Turn the drawer pulls from walnut and fasten them in place with a thin tenon fit into a mortise drilled into the drawer front.

BUILDING THE DRAWERS

1 Each drawer is custom-fit into its opening. First, plane the sides to the right height—one that permits them to slide into their openings with the least amount of clearance.

2 Cut dovetails using a backsaw and a coping saw. Use a paring chisel to achieve final fit.

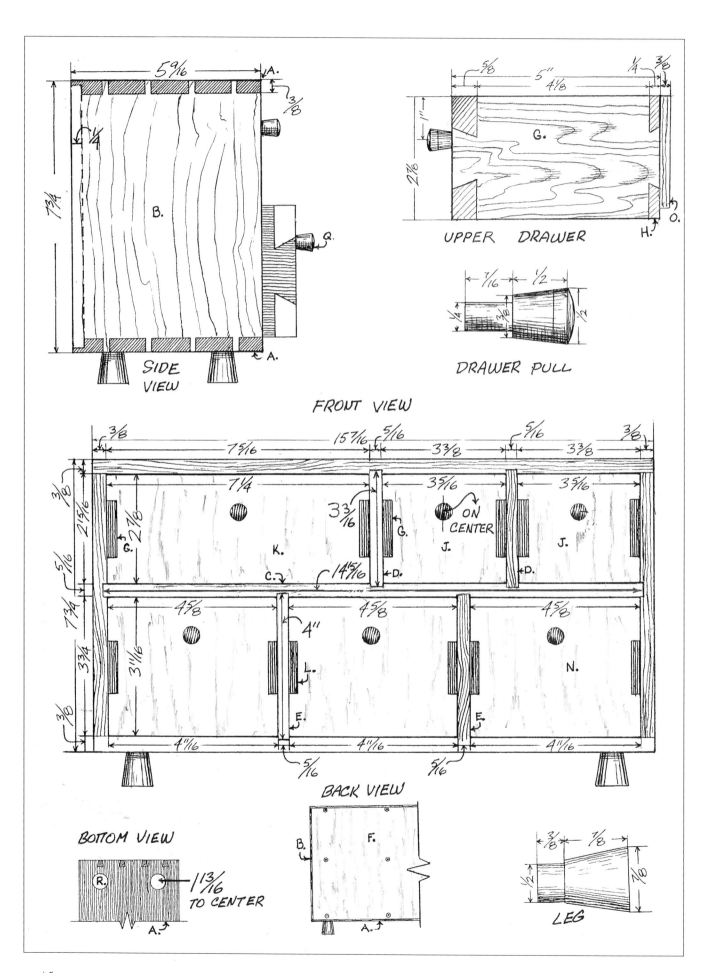

5 9/16

3/8

1/4

7 3/4

B.

A.

Q.

A.

SIDE
VIEW

5/8

5"

4 1/8

1/4

3/8

1"

G.

2 7/8

H.

O.

UPPER   DRAWER

7/16

1/2

1/4

3/8

1/2

DRAWER PULL

FRONT VIEW

3/8

7 5/16

15 7/16

5/16

5/16

3/8

3/8

3 3/8

3 3/8

2 15/16

7 1/4

3 3/16

3 5/16

3 5/16

2 7/8

G.

G.

K.

ON
CENTER

J.

J.

5/16

C.

14 15/16

D.

D.

7 3/4

4 5/8

4 5/8

4 5/8

3 11/16

4"

L.

N.

3 3/4

E.

E.

3/8

4 11/16

4 11/16

4 11/16

5/16

5/16

BACK VIEW

BOTTOM VIEW

R.

1 13/16
TO CENTER

A.

B.

F.

A.

3/8

7/8

1/2

7/8

LEG

BUILDING THE DRAWERS (CONTINUED)

3 After its parts have been cut and fit, the drawer is ready to assemble. Brads help the glue hold the drawer sides in place.

4 Note the surplus length at each corner. This is ground off with a belt sander.

5 After sanding the sides and the front of the drawer, slide the bottom into place and fasten with brads. Plug the holes at the ends of the grooves on both sides of the drawer front. Plane thickness from the two strips of softwood tacked to the back of each drawer to achieve final fit.

MATERIALS LIST

Case

A	Top and bottom	2 pcs.	$\frac{3}{8} \times 5\frac{9}{16} \times 15\frac{7}{16}$
B	End	2 pcs.	$\frac{3}{8} \times 5\frac{9}{16} \times 7\frac{3}{4}$
C	Central partition	1 pc.	$\frac{5}{16} \times 5\frac{1}{4} \times 14\frac{15}{16}$
D	Upper partition	2 pcs.	$\frac{5}{16} \times 5\frac{1}{4} \times 3\frac{3}{16}$
E	Lower partition	2 pcs.	$\frac{5}{16} \times 5\frac{1}{4} \times 4$
F	Back panel	1 pc.	$\frac{1}{4} \times 7\frac{1}{2} \times 15\frac{3}{16}$

Upper Drawers

G	Side	6 pcs.	$\frac{1}{4} \times 2\frac{7}{8} \times 5$
H	Short back	2 pcs.	$\frac{1}{4} \times 2\frac{3}{8} \times 3\frac{5}{16}$
I	Long back	1 pc.	$\frac{1}{4} \times 2\frac{3}{8} \times 7\frac{1}{4}$
J	Short front	2 pcs.	$\frac{5}{8} \times 2\frac{7}{8} \times 3\frac{5}{16}$
K	Long front	1 pc.	$\frac{5}{8} \times 2\frac{7}{8} \times 7\frac{1}{4}$

Lower Drawers

L	Side	6 pcs.	$\frac{1}{4} \times 3\frac{11}{16} \times 5$
M	Back	3 pcs.	$\frac{1}{4} \times 3\frac{3}{16} \times 4\frac{5}{8}$
N	Front	3 pcs.	$\frac{5}{8} \times 3\frac{11}{16} \times 4\frac{5}{8}$

Miscellaneous
Softwood fitting strip

O	Upper drawer	6 pcs.	$\frac{1}{4} \times \frac{3}{8} \times 2\frac{3}{8}$
P	Lower drawer	6 pcs.	$\frac{1}{4} \times \frac{3}{8} \times 3\frac{3}{16}$
Q	Pull	6 pcs.	$\frac{1}{2} \times 1$ (this includes tenon length)
R	Leg	4 pcs.	$\frac{7}{8} \times 1\frac{1}{4}$ (this includes tenon length)

*These are net measurements. A surplus should be added to dovetailed parts to allow them to be sanded flush.
*Opening measurements are given for drawer width and height. I subtract $\frac{1}{16}$ from both dimensions. This gives me $\frac{1}{32}$ clearance on all four sides of drawers.

CHEST BACK The back is unglued, fastened with screws to the case's top, bottom and central partitions.

BACK RABBET This photo shows the lapped rabbet corner at the back of the case.

21

CHIP BOX

Walnut, White Oak

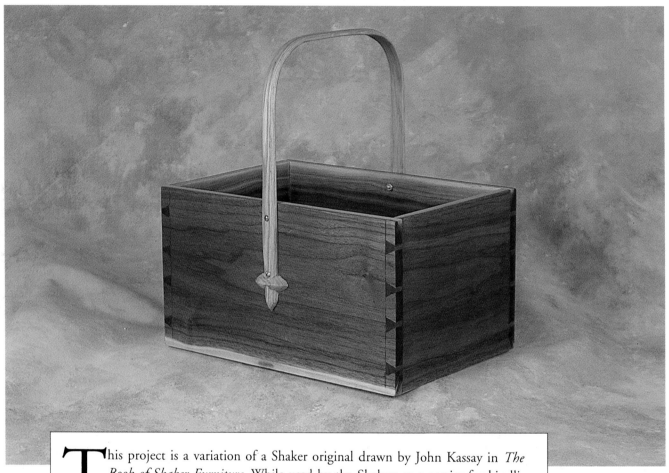

This project is a variation of a Shaker original drawn by John Kassay in *The Book of Shaker Furniture*. While used by the Shakers as a carrier for kindling and other fire-starting materials, in the modern home this piece might serve as a container for a child's crayons or markers, as a box for sewing notions, or as a basket for fruit or breads.

The drawknife and the spokeshave are not often found in the tool collections of contemporary woodworkers. Typically, in the modern shop, work that would once have been done with these hand tools is performed with the router or shaper, and while the drawknife and spokeshave clearly aren't suitable for every shaping operation, there are some tasks that can be accomplished more quickly and efficiently with these tools than with anything driven by an electric motor, and others that a router or a shaper can't perform at all.

The shaping of the bail (handle) on this chip box offers the contemporary woodworker a straightforward introduction to the use of these tools, although similar results can be achieved with rasps and files.

MAKING THE CHIP BOX

Walnut was used in the construction of this box with care taken to select pieces exhibiting contrasting streaks of white sapwood. The bail was shaped from white oak. While any of a number of woods would do nicely for the box, make the bail from a wood that is not only strong but also pliable enough to assume the *U* shape without breaking. Suitable woods include oaks, ashes and hickories.

Construction is very simple. After milling the stock to a thickness of ½″, rip the sides, ends and bottom to width and cut to length. Then plough a ¼″ × ¼″ groove in the sides and ends to receive the bottom. Then cut and pare dovetails to fit (see chapter twenty-five). With hand planes, bevel the edges of the bottom to allow them to slide in their grooves (see chapter one).

Then assemble the box and fit plugs into the ends of the grooves ploughed into the sides.

After removing the bail from its bending form, give its two paws their final shape using a paring chisel and a shop knife. Then fasten the bail to the box with four ⅛″ × 1¼″ brass machine screws and nuts.

SHAPING THE BAIL

1 The bail requires a ⅜″-thick length of continuous-grain bending stock. This means that, when viewed from the quarter-sawn side (the side with the narrow, parallel lines), the grain should run from end to end. Traditionally, this is achieved by splitting out the stock with the use of a froe and beetle. However, few contemporary woodworkers have these tools. You may, therefore, choose to use a length of sawn stock selected for straight grain.

Before bending, work the band-sawn strip with a drawknife and spokeshave to rough-in the desired shape. At this point, it isn't necessary to be fussy. The goal is simply to round the edges on the top side of the bail since this procedure can be carried out more comfortably now, when the stock is unbent, than later, when the bail has taken on its *U* shape.

STEAM BENDING

1 My steamer is a deep fat fryer. I've cut an opening in the lid the same size as the outside diameter of a length of PVC which I use as a steam chamber. Three sheet metal screws turned into the PVC just above its base are allowed to protrude. These rest on the fryer's lid holding the steam chamber above the water's surface. A square of hardware cloth that laps the bottom of the steam chamber and is screwed to the PVC supports the material being steamed. To hold the entire apparatus upright, a strip of wood lath is screwed to the PVC and spring-clamped to a stepladder.

Similarly, functional steamers can be made in a number of different ways. Many woodworkers use a hot plate and a tea kettle with a spout fitted with a length of plastic hose which conducts steam to a chamber of some sort—a wooden box, a length of downspout, or a section of PVC.

Steam the bending stock long enough to become plastic. In my steamer, with material of this thickness, that means about forty-five minutes.

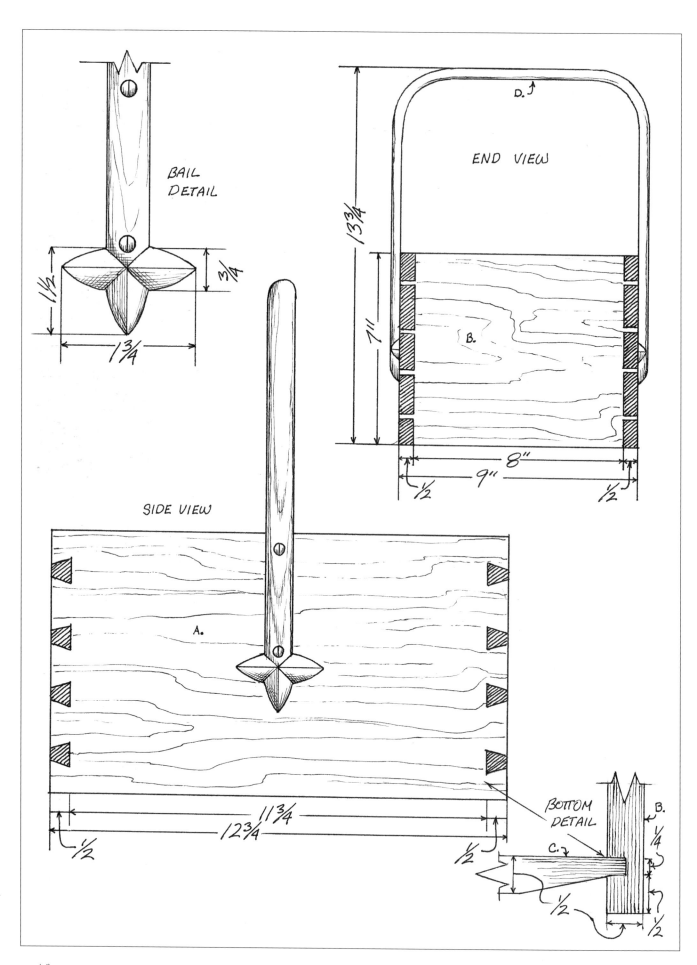

BAIL
DETAIL

1½

¾

1¾

END VIEW

D.

13¾

7"

B.

8"

9"

½

½

SIDE VIEW

A.

B.

12¾

11¾

½

½

BOTTOM
DETAIL

B.

¼

C.

½

½

STEAM BENDING (CONTINUED)

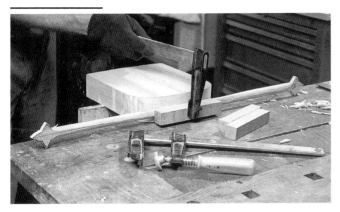

2 Prepare bending forms beforehand. This particular form, a 2″-thick block of poplar cut to the inside profile of the bail, is nailed to a block of wood held in a vise. Necessary clamps and clamping blocks are placed nearby. Gloves are needed because the steamed oak will be very hot when removed from the steam chamber.

Although you shouldn't rush, proceed quickly because the steamed wood will cool rapidly, becoming less pliable.

Place the midway point along the length of the oak strip at the halfway point across the width of the poplar form. Then clamp it, using a block of wood to protect the oak from clamp marks.

3 Bend the oak strip into its *U* shape, holding it in place with a second clamp set perpendicular to the first. Again, use blocks of scrap to protect the oak. From above, the strip can be seen to have assumed the shape of the bail.

Green wood is best for bending, but dry material can be coaxed into the required shapes with enough steam and enough patience.

Wood bending, particularly bending involving the sharp curves shown here, is a process rich with opportunities for failure. Sometimes, even after selecting continuous-grained material, even after steaming that material thoroughly, fracture can occur along the bends. When that happens, the only solution is to start the process all over again.

SHAVING TOOLS

Shown are the shaving tools I use in my shop. The two with turned wooden handles are drawknives. The knife at the top is a general-purpose tool, while the one at the bottom is a variety known as the "inshave" used by makers of Windsor chairs to hollow-out seats. The two middle tools are metal-bodied spokeshaves. The shave with the straight iron is used for general-purpose work, while the other, a hollow shave, can only be used for rounding spindles.

MATERIALS LIST

A	Side	2 pcs.	½ × 7 × 12¾
B	End	2 pcs.	½ × 7 × 9
C	Bottom	1 pc.	½ × 8½ × 12¼
D	Bail	1 pc.	⅜ × 2⅛ × 29
E	Plug	4 pcs.	¼ × ¼ × ¼, shaved to fit
F	Machine screws & nuts	4 pcs.	⅛ × 1¼

These are net measurements. Surplus should be added to lengths of dovetailed sides and ends to allow joints to be sanded flush.

22

PEGGED DISPLAY SHELF

Curly Maple, Walnut

In the strictest sense, the word *figured* describes the pattern of color and markings visible on the surface of all lumber; however in common usage, the word is reserved for boards exhibiting particularly dramatic patterns.

Curly figure, which consists of bars of rippling grain, is not uncommon in maple and is also present in walnut, cherry, oak and other species.

Bird's eye, another variety of figured maple, is identified not by bars of rippling grain but instead by a swirling pattern dimpled with tiny dots.

The pegged display shelf shown here has a top shelf, a lower shelf, and two turned pegs made of bird's eye maple.

MAKING THE
PEGGED DISPLAY SHELF

After the material has been dimensioned, profile the end panels, the back panels, and the lower shelf on the band saw. Form the moulded edge on the top on a shaper or table-mounted router fit with appropriate cutters.

Next, cut joinery. You can cut the stopped rabbet that will house the ends of the back panel on the table saw (see chapter five), with a table-mounted router, or by hand, using chisels.

Cut the through mortises in the end panels (see chapter twelve). Then, with a backsaw or a stack of dado cutters on the table saw, cut the tenons on the ends of the lower shelf and pare to fit these mortises.

On the lathe, turn the two Shaker-style pegs. Then, fit their tenons into mortises drilled into the shelf's back panel.

When all the parts have been dry-assembled and checked for fit, glue the frame and screw it together. Install the top, using four 1″ no. 6 wood screws passing through the top into the end grain of the side panels. Glue four maple plugs and tap them into the countersunk screw holes.

FIGURED LANGUAGE

In *The Woodworker's Dictionary* by Englishman Vic Taylor, the word *curl* is defined this way: "Highly figured grain obtained by cutting through the junction of a tree or large limb. Used only in veneer form. Also known as crotch or feather."

If you ordered curly material from an American supplier of figured wood, you would not get the material described by Vic Taylor. You would, instead, get lumber marked by rippling bars of grain marching across the widths of the boards perpendicular to the grain direction. This inconsistency of language occurs not only among dealers working in different countries but also among dealers in the U.S.

One of the sawmill operators from whom I buy has his own system of figured wood classification: If it tears out in the planer, it's curly. Period. And he sells it that way. Because I've bought from him in the past and am aware of his system of classification, I carefully inspect every curly board I buy from him, but a customer unfamiliar with his system might assume that whatever he purchased from this sawmill operator as curly would exhibit a figure that was consistent from board to board and consistent with the buyer's expectation of curly lumber.

In general I've found that owner/operators of small sawmills aren't good sources of figured lumber. In part, this may be because they are sawyers, not woodworkers, and therefore look at lumber from a different perspective. But I also think that owner/operators of small sawmills don't have the experience with figured lumber to make considered judgments about its quality.

My advice? Buy from the experts. Yes, you will pay a bit more for your curly maple than you would if you bought it from the guy down the road who owns a portable sawmill, but you're much more likely to get the kind of material you want. And there are experts in this field, people who buy and sell figured lumber every day, and their names can be found in the advertising

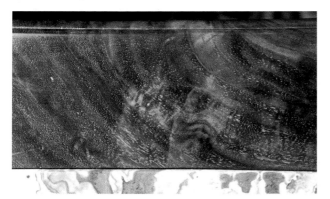

1 The border of the chess table (featured in chapter three) shows the kind of figuring common in crotch-grained lumber.

2 Tiny dots are scattered across the surface of this piece of bird's eye maple. (This grain is used on the top of the display shelf in this chapter.)

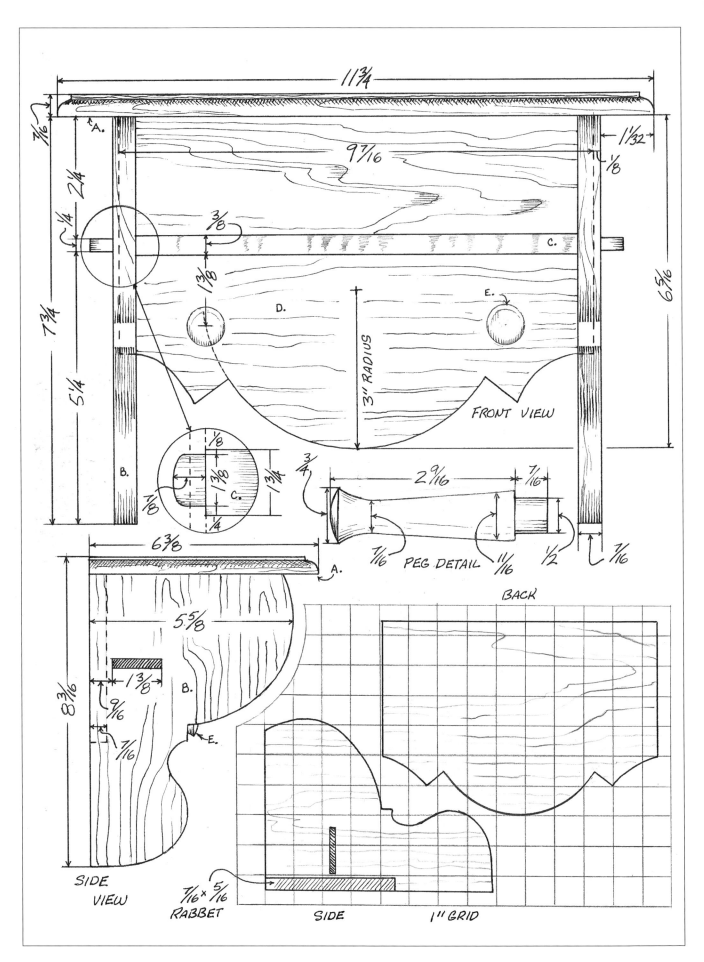

11 3/4

7/16

2 1/4

1/4

A.

9 9/16

1 1/32

1/8

3/8

1 3/8

D.

E.

3" RADIUS

C.

6 5/16

7 3/4

5 1/4

B.

1/8

1/8

1 3/100

1 3/4

C.

1/4

3/4

2 9/16

7/16

7/16

PEG DETAIL

11/16

1/2

7/16

6 3/8

A.

FRONT VIEW

BACK

5 5/8

8 3/16

1 3/8

B.

9/16

7/16

E.

SIDE
VIEW

7/16 × 5/16
RABBET

SIDE

1" GRID

section of any woodworking magazine. Listed below are the phone numbers of two such specialists:

Island Hardwoods 1-910-278-1169

Sandy Pond Hardwoods 1-800-546-9663

Here, too, is a list of definitions for some of the terms commonly applied to figured wood:

- **Tiger maple.** Often referred to by the generic "curly," the wood identified by this term includes the soft (red and silver) curly maples.
- **Fiddleback maple.** This material, characterized by a tighter, more compact curl than is evident in tiger maple, comes from hard maple and is widely used by violin makers for the backs of their instruments.
- **Blistered maple.** This figure, which is also present in hard maple, has a surface on which there is the appearance of raised blisters or boils.

- **Quilted maple.** A product of the western big-leaf maple, this material is marked by a regular pattern of what appear to be raised areas of varying shapes.
- **Bird's eye maple.** This variety of hard maple exhibits swirling grain scattered with dots resembling bird's eyes.
- **Crotch-grained.** For American woodworkers, this is the material about which Vic Taylor wrote in his definition of "curly." Sometimes known as "feathered," this is taken from the junction of a tree and a large limb.
- **Burl.** Taken from growths that appear on the trunks of certain trees, this material is highly prized by makers of veneer and by turners for its wildly convoluted grain.

3 This panel of glued-up cherry exhibits a wavy figure not uncommon in cherry (see the side table in chapter seven for an excellent example).

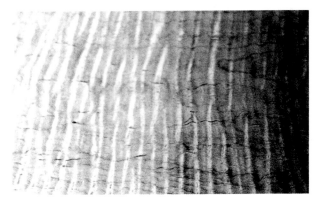

4 This photo shows a length of heavily figured curly (tiger) maple (featured in the document chest in chapter twenty-five).

SUSTAINABLE FORESTS

At some point, everyone who applies tools to wood considers the issue of forest maintenance. Although many experts believe that reserves of the commonly used American species are adequate to meet projected needs, there is an irrefutable difference in the quality of available material. Although cherry, maple and oak are always on hand in any well-stocked lumberyard, the boards are not as wide and not as clear as they were even a single generation in the past. And the situation is even more critical for walnut, the king of American hardwoods. Walnut saw logs are increasingly rare, and when they can be found of any quality, they are inevitably snatched up by veneer mills.

More information about this problem and its possible solutions can be had by writing to the National Arbor Day Foundation at the following address:

The National Arbor Day Foundation

100 Arbor Avenue

Nebraska City NE 68410

MATERIALS LIST			
A	Top	1 pc.	$7/16 \times 6\frac{3}{8} \times 11\frac{3}{4}$
B	End	2 pcs.	$7/16 \times 5\frac{5}{8} \times 7\frac{3}{4}$
C	Shelf	1 pc.	$3/8 \times 1\frac{3}{4} \times 10\frac{1}{2}$
D	Back	1 pc.	$7/16 \times 6\frac{5}{16} \times 9\frac{7}{16}$
E	Peg	2 pcs.	$3/4 \times 3$
F	Plug	4 pcs.	$3/8 \times 1/4$
G	Screws	various	

23
TABLETOP DESK

Cherry, Poplar

W e live in an age of highly specialized home furnishings. We have tables on which we prepare food, other tables at which we eat it, still others from which we serve it. We have desks at which we do our writing and figuring, other desks at which we work at our computers. In eighteenth- and nineteenth-century American homes, in which there was often less space available for specialized pieces and in which there was often less disposable income for their purchase, furniture often served multiple functions.

A nightstand might double as a washstand. Food might be prepared at a table which was later used for dining. In some cases, cleverly designed accessories were necessary to make this flexibility possible. The tabletop desk shown here is one example.

Created to be placed upon a table that might otherwise be used for dining, food preparation, or holding a wash basin, the desk—described by John Kassay in *The Book of Shaker Furniture*—is a completely equipped writing station, with a tiny inkwell drawer, a till for pens and pencils, and a large drawer for stationery.

DESIGNED BY

JIM PIERCE

MAKING THE TABLETOP DESK

After the material has been dimensioned, edge-joint and glue the boards that will make up the desk top.

Plough a ⅛″ × ¼″ groove on the inside faces of the desk sides, front, and back. This groove will later receive the bottom of the materials compartment. Then, cut openings in the sides for the inkwell and stationery drawers.

Next, cut the angles on the desk sides on the band saw, after which the four sides of the case are dovetailed. The case is dry-assembled, and the bevels on the top edge of the front and back are marked from the angles on the sides. Form these bevels with a hand plane, and glue-up the four walls of the case around the bottom of the materials compartment.

Before installing the bottom, glue and brad into place the cock bead that frames the stationery drawer. Also at this time, glue the two fill strips that will guide the stationery drawer in position. Then, tack the bottom into place using small finishing nails. Nails are perhaps better than screws for this particular application because they are flexible enough to allow for seasonal expansion and contraction of the bottom across its width. Screws—unless they pass through oversized holes which would be very difficult to

achieve in such thin stock—could lock the material so that cracking would occur in connection with this expansion and contraction.

The inkwell drawer is next. The unusually shaped long drawer side does two things. First, it is a drawer guide, and second, it prevents the drawer (with its bottle of ink) from being completely withdrawn from the case, a circumstance that could easily have had messy results.

After forming the drawer parts, glue and tack them together. Then, fit the drawer to its opening and screw the wooden bracket that acts as its guide and keeper to the inside face of the desk back.

Assemble the stationery drawer with through dovetails at the front and half-blind dovetails at the back.

The till rests on a pair of ⅛″-thick supports which are glued to the inside faces of the desk front and back. After installing these supports, glue the till—with its side already glued to the bottom—into place atop the supports. Fasten it also to the desk side with a thin line of glue.

The top panel is removed from the clamps and planed to a thickness of ⁵⁄₁₆″. Then, cut ⅛″ × ⅛″ grooves in both ends of the top panel to receive the tongues on the breadboard ends. Form and fit the tongues to the grooves. Hold

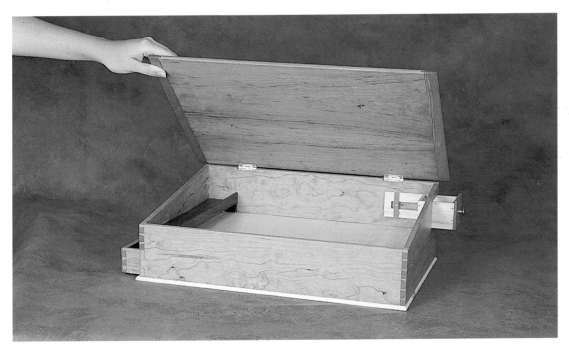

The opened tabletop desk reveals the ink well drawer and the paper drawer in the bottom.

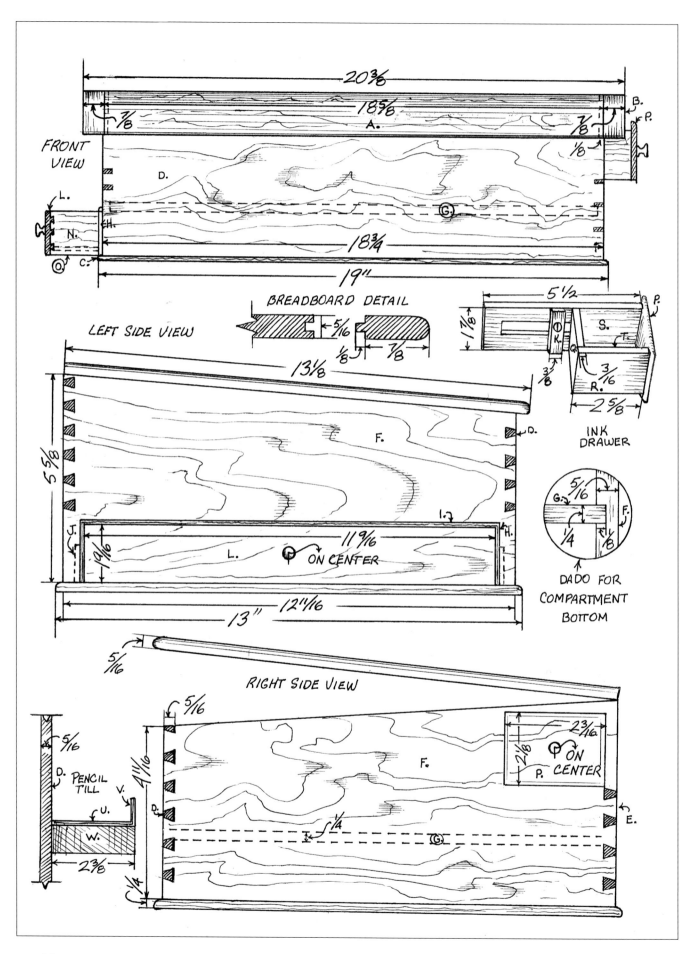

20⅜

18⅝

A.

⅞

B.

P.

FRONT
VIEW

⅛

D.

⅛

L.

H.

G.

N.

18¾

Q.

C.

19"

BREADBOARD DETAIL

5/16

⅛

⅞

5½

P.

1⅞

S.

K.

Q.

T.

⅜

R.

3/16

2⅝

INK
DRAWER

LEFT SIDE VIEW

13⅛

D.

5⅝

F.

5/16

G.

F.

¼

⅛

DADO FOR
COMPARTMENT
BOTTOM

J.

1 9/16

L.

11 9/16

ON CENTER

I.

H.

12 11/16

13"

RIGHT SIDE VIEW

5/16

5/16

5/16

4 1/16

D. PENCIL
TILL

V.

U.

W.

2⅜

¼

D.

F.

¼

G.

2 3/16

2⅛

P.

ON
CENTER

E.

each breadboard end in place with a dab of glue on the tongue at the middle of the tongue's length. The remainder of the tongue floats on the groove, allowing for seasonal expansion and contraction of the top.

Hinges are problems because of the top's extreme thinness. My dad, who built this particular piece, struggled to find screws that could get a good enough bite in the top to hold it in place. After trying and discarding several brass screws, he settled on deep-threaded ⅜" no. 6 steel screws from which he'd ground away the tips so that they wouldn't penetrate the upper surface of the top.

After fitting the hinges, remove the hardware, and give the desk a final sanding.

KILN-DRIED OR AIR-DRIED

Reference books inevitably cite the necessity of using kiln-dried material for funiture construction.

I think that's misleading.

Of the thousands of board feet of lumber I've turned into chairs and into casework, less than a quarter was kiln-dried. The remainder was air-dired outdoors and finish-dried in my shop. Nevertheless, I can remember only two occasions when pieces I built experienced wood failure.

Once, I built a Hepplewhite huntboard from air-dried cherry. The top (which didn't fail) was fastened to cleats fixed with slotted screw holes. But one of the end panels, which I had triple-tenoned into the posts, split after sitting in our living room through a couple of cold, dry Ohio winters. In looking back on the construction of the huntboard, I remember hurrying to finish it before Christmas since it was a present for my wife.

When I glued up the end panels, I remember noticing, as I slathered glue on the middle tenon, that I hadn't cut the top and bottom tenons back to allow the end panel to shrink. Each tenon completely filled its mortise. But the glue was already on the middle tenon and in its mortise. To cut the other tenons back, I would have to wash away the glue, find my paring chisel, pare the tenons, and reglue. Or risk having the aliphatic resin glue set before the joint was assembled. I remember thinking it wasn't worth the effort. I remember thinking I could get away with it.

The end panel failed because I built it to fail.

I think that if allowances are made during design for the inevitable movement of wood, carefully air-dried material is every bit as good as kiln-dried. In fact, I think that careful air-drying is preferable to the kind of rushed kiln-drying practiced by some commercial driers. At least in humid Ohio, air-drying is a gradual process during which wood surrenders its mosture so slowly that surface checking is almost unheard of. And it's worth mentioning that, just like air-dried stock, kiln-dried stock, when exposed to humid, July conditions, quickly takes on enough moisture to reach 11, 12 or even 13 percent.

The answer to the problem of wood movement isn't laboring to make wood inert; it is, I think, to accept movement as an inevitable component of solid-wood construction and to design to accommodate that inevitability.

MATERIALS LIST

Desk			
A	Top	1 pc.	5⁄16 × 13⅛ × 18⅝
B	Breadboard end	2 pcs.	5⁄16 × 1 × 13⅛
C	Bottom	1 pc.	¼ × 13 × 1
D	Front	1 pc.	5⁄16 × 4 11⁄16 × 18¾
E	Back	1 pc.	5⁄16 × 5⅝ × 18¾
F	Side	2 pcs.	5⁄16 × 5⅝ × 12 11⁄16
G	Compartment bottom	1 pc.	¼ × 12 5⁄16 × 18⅜
H	Short cock bead	2 pcs.	⅛ × ½ × 1⅞
I	Long cock bead	1 pc.	⅛ × ½ × 11⅞
J	Drawer fill strip	2 pcs.	⅛ × 1 × 16¼
K	Ink-drawer stop	1 pc.	⅜ × ⅜ × 1⅞
Stationery drawer			
L	Front	1 pc.	5⁄16 × 1 9⁄16 × 11 9⁄16
M	Back	1 pc.	¼ × 1 9⁄16 × 11 9⁄16
N	Side	2 pcs.	¼ × 1 9⁄16 × 18
O	Bottom	1 pc.	¼ × 11 5⁄16 × 18¼
Ink drawer			
P	Front	1 pc.	5⁄16 × 2⅛ × 2 13⁄16
Q	Back	1 pc.	3⁄16 × 1⅞ × 2 3⁄32
R	Short side	1 pc.	3⁄16 × 1⅞ × 2⅝
S	Long side	1 pc.	3⁄16 × 1⅞ × 5½
T	Bottom	1 pc.	3⁄16 × 2 11⁄32 × 2½
Pencil till			
U	Bottom	1 pc.	⅛ × 2¼ × 12 1⁄16
V	Side	1 pc.	⅛ × ¾ × 12 1⁄16
W	Support	2 pcs.	⅛ × ¾ × 2⅜
Hardware			
X	Hinge	2 pcs.	1½ × ⅞
Y	Pull	2 pcs.	½ × ½
Z	Screws and nails	various	

**These are net measurements. A surplus should be added to dovetailed parts to allow them to be sanded flush.*

**Pulls were ordered from Constantine's Hardware.*

24

SHERATON-STYLE TABLE

Walnut, White Pine

Several years ago, a customer asked if I could
design a telephone table. She wanted something
small with a single drawer just large enough for
a telephone book. I showed her photos of several tables
I'd made (including the Hepplewhite-style end table
pictured in this book), but nothing in the photos
pleased her.

A week later, I showed her a half-dozen very rough
sketches of various one-drawer tables. Among them
was one with several features I'd borrowed from Sheraton originals, specifically the tiptoe feet and the round
post meeting the flat apron. She took one look at the
sketches, pointed at one, and said, "That's it."

This is the table she picked.

MAKING THE SHERATON-STYLE TABLE

Begin construction with the legs. The exact shapes of their various sections can be determined by the individual woodworker; however, the section that will be joined to the apron, that section above the upper bead, must be carefully formed so that it maintains a consistent diameter from top to bottom as any variation in diameter will show itself here as a gap.

Once a leg has been formed but before it's taken from the lathe, mark the centerlines for the mortises that will receive the apron tenons. Do this using the lathe's indexing head.

The indexing head is a disk centered on the lathe's axis with holes drilled near its perimeter. Each of these holes marks 10° of the disk's 360° circumference and, by extension, 10° of the 360° circumference of any work centered on the lathe's axis. After selecting the faces of the leg that will be visible from the table's side and end, the tool rest is brought into contact with that section of the leg that will be joined to the apron. The indexing head is then locked at this position (on my lathe that's simply a matter of releasing a spring-loaded peg into one of the holes drilled near the head's circumference) and a line is drawn along the tool rest on the leg. Then, using the spring-loaded peg to count holes, the work is turned nine stops on the indexing head which is then locked at this point and a second line drawn. These lines are 90° apart and mark the centerlines of the mortises that will house the apron tenons.

After the apron parts and drawer rails have been dimensioned, cut their tenons. You can start this on the table saw, but it must be completed by hand or on the band saw as the shoulders of the apron parts must be undercut so that the shoulders come to a sharp point. This is necessary if the shoulders are to make tight contact with the round surface of the leg.

The table frame—consisting of the four legs, the three sections of the apron, and the two drawer rails—is then glued-up.

Next, install drawer runners and kicker strips. The kicker strips on this table serve two purposes. First, they keep the drawer properly aligned when it is partially open. Second, they act as cleats to affix the table's top to its base. In order

to accommodate the seasonal expansion and contraction of the top across its width, the screws that fasten the top to the base should pass through oversized holes in the kicker strips.

Drawer construction is tricky in one respect. Like the parts of the apron and the drawer rails, the drawer front must be shaped to allow it to be closed so that its surface is flush with the surface of the drawer rails without wide gaps at either side. Like the apron and drawer rail shoulders, the drawer front could be undercut, but I wanted a more graceful shape in this location because it is visible when the drawer is opened. I decided then to curve the back side of the drawer front, matching it to the curve on the legs.

After fitting the drawer, sand and finish the table and drawer.

MATERIALS LIST

Table

A	Top	1 pc.	$\frac{3}{4} \times 17 \times 23\frac{1}{2}$
B	Leg	4 pcs.	$2\frac{7}{16} \times 2\frac{7}{16} \times 23$
C	Apron side		$\frac{7}{8} \times 5\frac{1}{8} \times 18\frac{3}{4}$ (includes $\frac{7}{8}$ tenon on
		2 pcs.	each end)
D	Apron end		$\frac{7}{8} \times 5\frac{1}{8} \times 12\frac{1}{4}$ (with
		1 pc.	tenons)
E	Top drawer rail		$\frac{7}{8} \times 1\frac{1}{4} \times 12\frac{1}{4}$
		1 pc.	(with tenons)
F	Bottom drawer rail		$\frac{7}{8} \times \frac{7}{8} \times 12\frac{1}{4}$
		1 pc.	(with tenons)
G	Kicker strip	2 pcs.	$1\frac{1}{4} \times 1\frac{1}{2} \times 17\frac{7}{8}$
H	Drawer runner	2 pcs.	$\frac{7}{8} \times \frac{7}{8} \times 17\frac{7}{8}$

Drawer

I	Drawer front	1 pc.	$\frac{7}{8} \times 2\frac{15}{16} \times 10\frac{1}{2}$
J	Drawer back	1 pc.	$\frac{1}{2} \times 2\frac{15}{16} \times 10$
K	Drawer side	2 pcs.	$\frac{1}{2} \times 2\frac{15}{16} \times 17$

Hardware

L	Brass knob	1 pc.	$\frac{1}{2} \times \frac{1}{2}$
M	Screws	various	

These are net measurements. A surplus should be added to dovetailed parts to allow them to be sanded flush.
Pull was ordered from Constantine's Hardware.

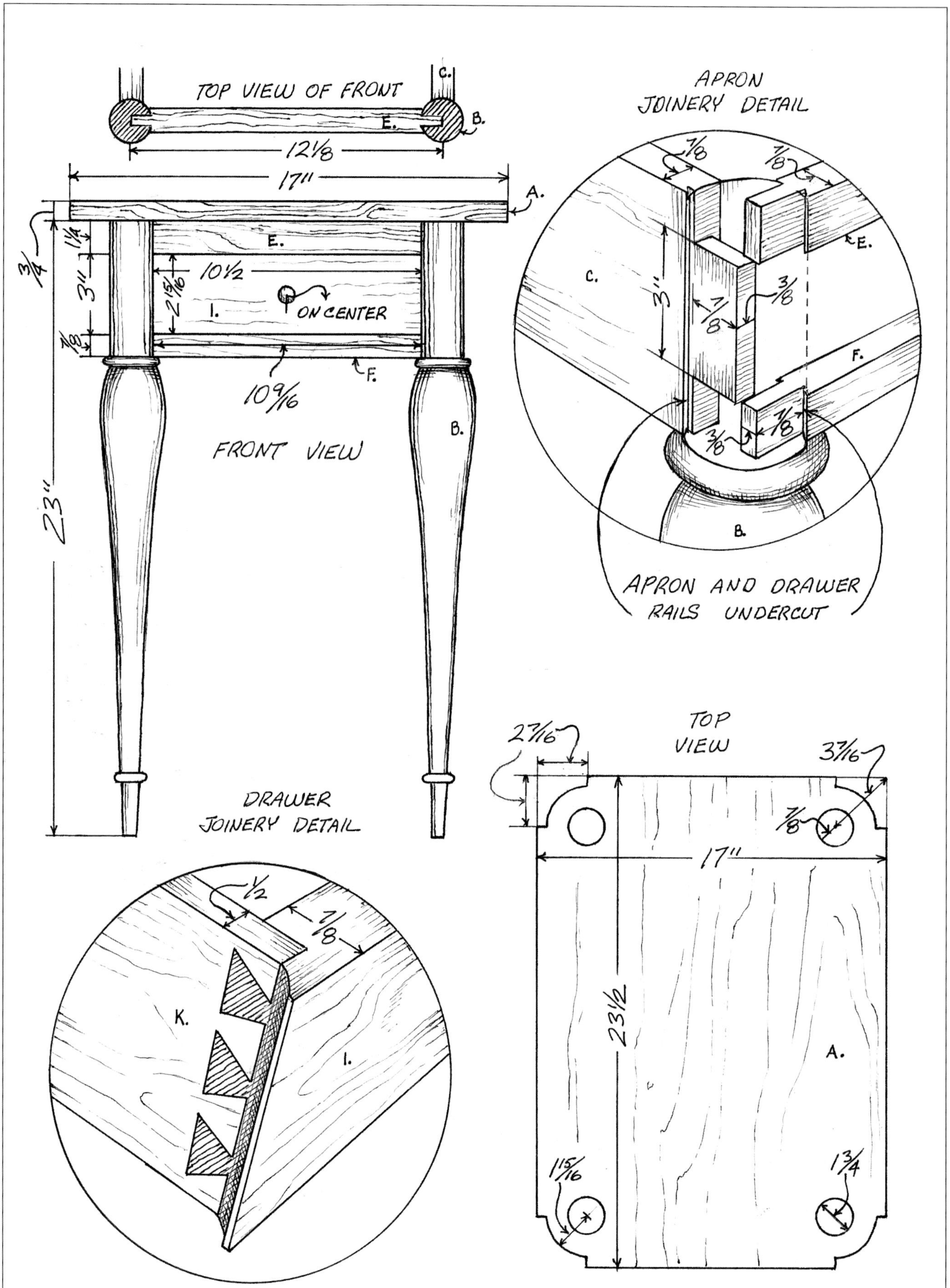
TOP VIEW OF FRONT
C.
B.
E.
12 1/8
17"
A.
3/4
1 1/4
3"
1/8
E.
10 1/2
2 15/16
I.
ON CENTER
10 9/16
F.
B.
FRONT VIEW
23"
APRON
JOINERY DETAIL
7/8
7/8
E.
C.
3"
3/8
7/8
F.
3/8
7/8
B.
APRON AND DRAWER
RAILS UNDERCUT
DRAWER
JOINERY DETAIL
1/2
7/8
K.
I.
TOP
VIEW
2 7/16
3 7/16
7/8
17"
23 1/2
A.
1 15/16
1 3/4

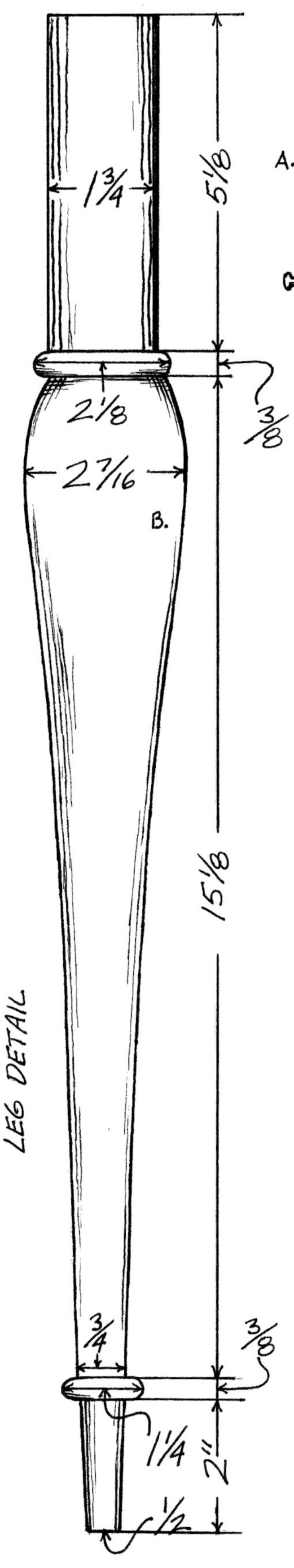
LEG DETAIL
1 3/4
5 1/8
2 1/8
3/8
2 7/16
B.
15 1/8
3/4
3/8
1 1/4
2"
1/2

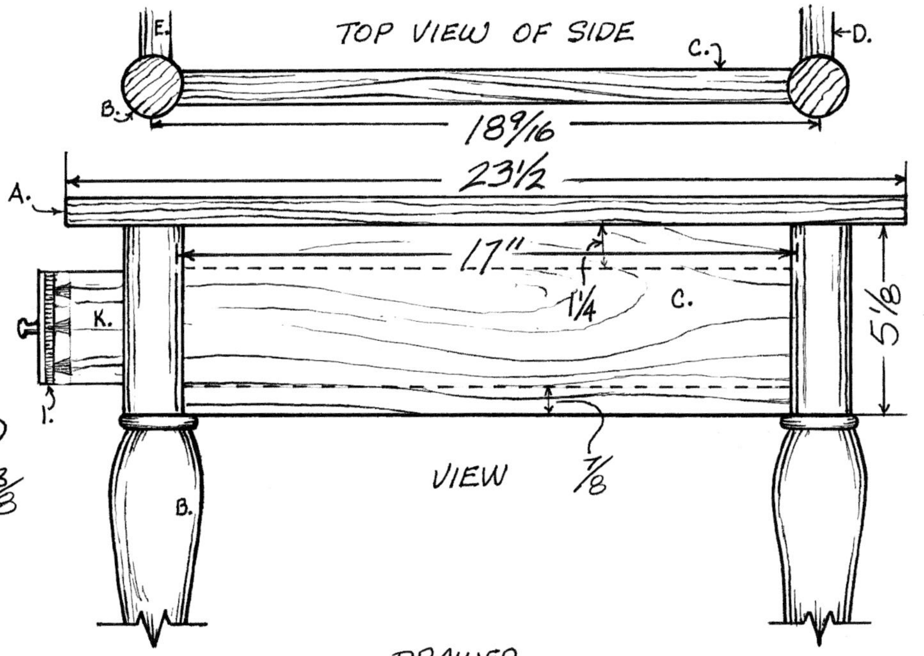
TOP VIEW OF SIDE
E.
D.
C.
B.
18 9/16
23 1/2
A.
17"
1 1/4
C.
K.
I.
5 1/8
7/8
VIEW
B.

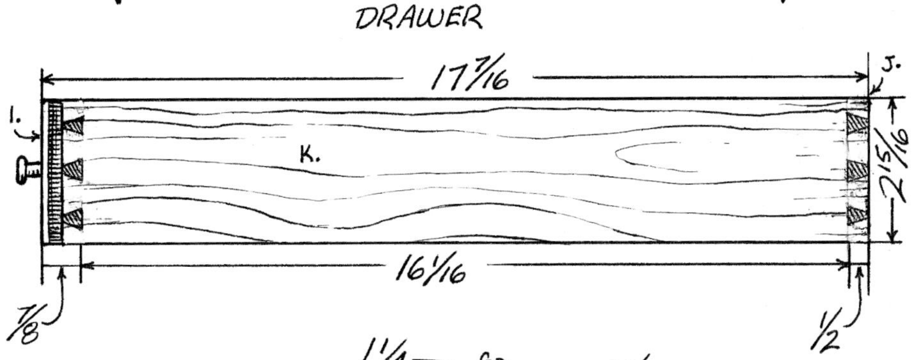
DRAWER
17 7/16
J.
I.
K.
2 15/16
16 1/16
7/8
1/2

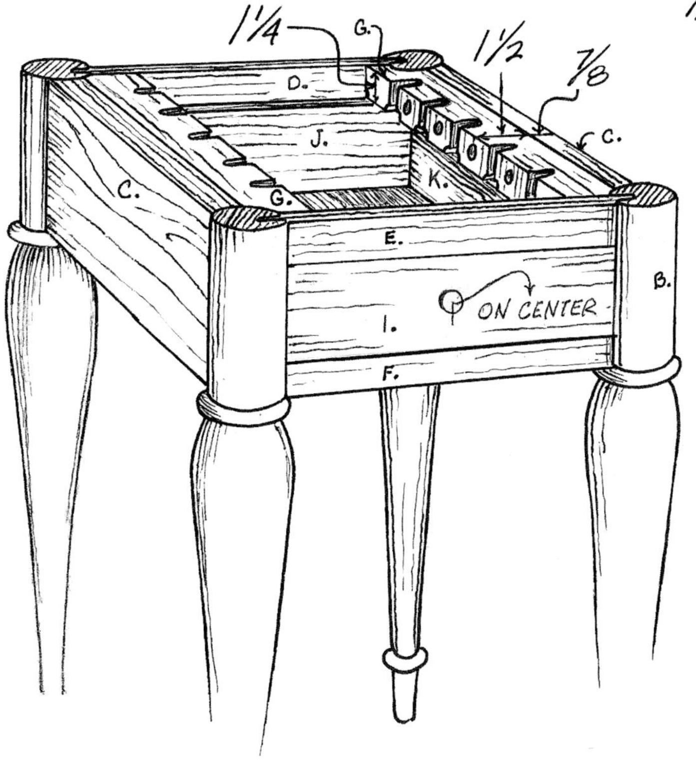
1 1/4
G.
1 1/2
7/8
D.
C.
J.
C.
K.
G.
E.
B.
ON CENTER
I.
F.

25

DOCUMENT CHEST

Curly Maple, White Pine

In spite of their well-known affection for plainness, Shaker craftsmen often employed heavily figured wood in their furniture. There are, for example, many Shaker chairs, tables, and chests fashioned, wholly or in part, from curly maple.

This marriage of simple forms and figured wood produced some of the most appealing examples of American woodwork. Unlike ornate Chippendale pieces built of figured wood which can sometime overwhelm the observer, the clean plainness of Shaker furniture provides a comfortable setting for the display of such material.

Although the original of this document chest (described by John Kassay in *The Book of Shaker Furniture*) was built of pine, I chose curly maple for this example hoping to be rewarded with another happy marriage.

MAKING THE DOCUMENT CHEST

After the stock has been thicknessed, ripped to width, and cut to length, plough a ¼″ × ⅜″ groove on the inside faces of the front, back and two ends. This groove will receive the raised panel that will separate the upper storage chamber from the drawer compartment.

Then cut through dovetails for the four corners of the case (this process is detailed in the sidebar below). Glue the joints and assemble the case around the raised panel that separates its two sections.

Shape the moulded edge on the top and bottom of the lid and on the top side of the chest's bottom. Fasten the bottom to the case with ten 1½″ no. 10 wood screws. These pass through oversized holes drilled in the bottom to allow for seasonal expansion and contraction across its width.

Although the Shaker original didn't have them, I installed a pair of sturdy ash cleats on the underside of the lid to prevent it from cupping—a problem I encountered the first time I built one of these chests.

Build the drawer next (see the sidebar below) with through dovetails at the rear and half-blind dovetails at the

front. Slide the drawer bottom into its groove and tack it up into the drawer back. Then fit the length of the completed drawer by planing thickness from a pair of softwood strips tacked to the back side of the drawer.

Complete the chest by finishing the wood and installing the hardware.

CUTTING DOVETAILS BY HAND

There's something soothing about the process of cutting dovetails by hand. The shop is quiet. The air is clean, carrying no load of machine-generated dust. There is the sense that this is what woodworking is supposed to be: calm, unhurried, not driven by the frantic scream and whine of power tools. This is woodworking stripped of the efficient unpleasantness of technology, reduced to the application of sharp tools to beautiful material.

Even though the case must be made first, the following discussion of hand-cut dovetails will begin with drawer construction because, unlike the case, the drawer requires the creation of both through and half-blind dovetails.

1 The process begins with careful stock preparation. After the parts have been dimensioned, cut the grooves into which the drawer bottom will slide. Establish base-

lines for every pin and tail (the pins are those parts of the dovetail joint that fit between the tails). Score these lines across the grain with either a marking gauge or a sharp knife. In the case of the through dovetails (those on the back of the drawer), lines should be placed a distance from the end that is ¹⁄₁₆″ more than the thickness of the stock to which the piece is being joined. Since, in this case, the drawer sides and back are ½″ thick, the baselines will be set ⁹⁄₁₆″ from the ends of the drawer sides and back. Placement of the baselines on the front end of the drawer sides is handled a little differently because these joints will be half-blind dovetails. Because the drawer front is ¹¹⁄₁₆″ thick, set the baselines on the front ends of the drawer sides ½″ from the end. This leaves ³⁄₁₆″ of drawer-front material covering the ends of the dovetails on the front ends of the drawer sides.

2 Cut the tails first. After deciding on their widths, use pencil lines (drawn with the aid of a try square) to mark the end grain of the drawer side. These

lines indicate the widths of the gaps between the widest parts of the tails.

At this point, you can mark the actual angles of the tails

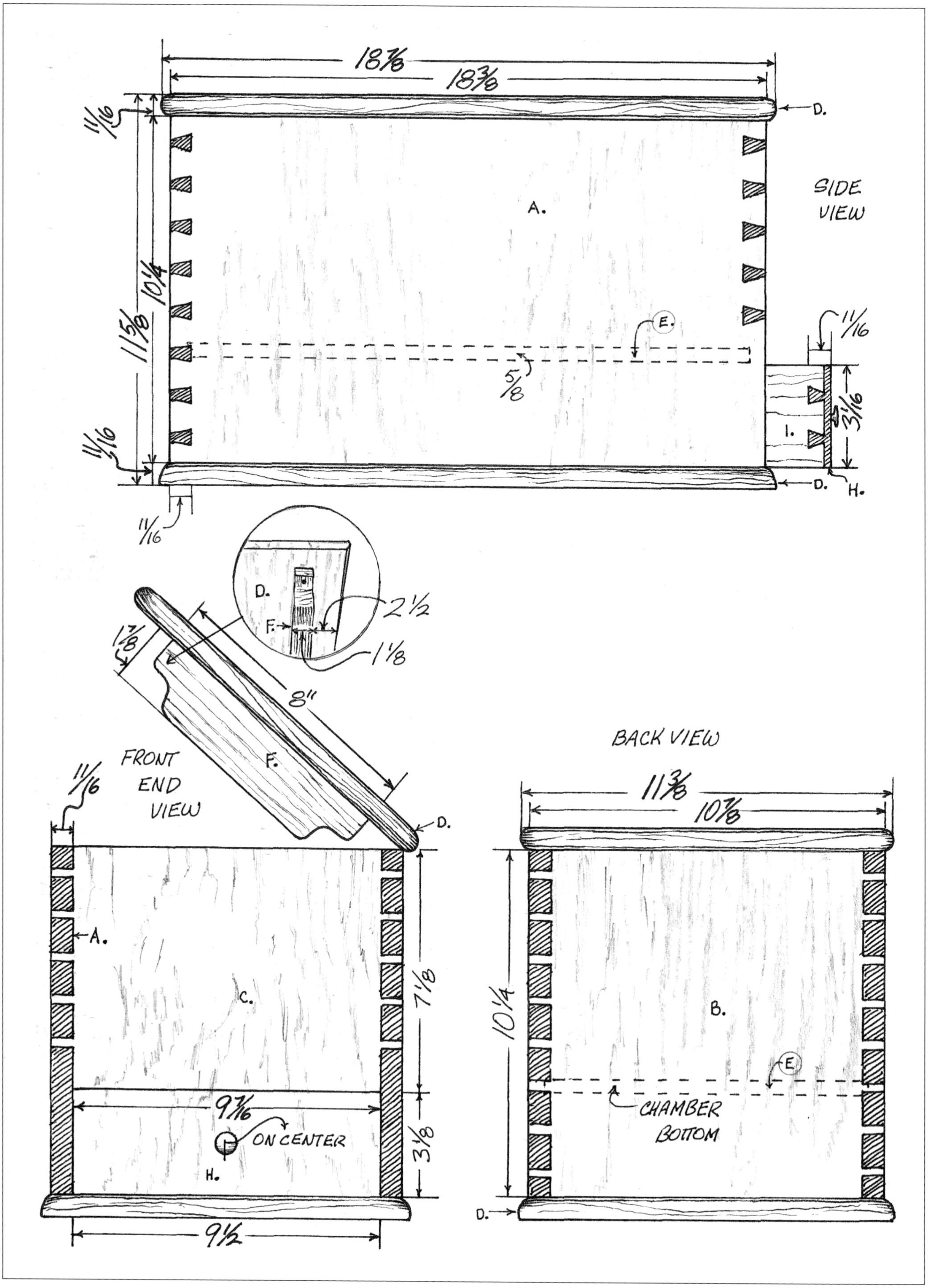
18 7/8
18 3/8
11/16
D.
SIDE VIEW
A.
10 1/4
11 5/8
E.
5/8
11/16
3 1/16
I.
D.
H.
11/16
D.
F.
2 1/2
1 1/8
1 7/8
8"
F.
D.
FRONT END VIEW
11/16
A.
C.
7 1/8
9 7/16
ON CENTER
H.
3 1/8
9 1/2
BACK VIEW
11 3/8
10 7/8
10 1/4
B.
E.
CHAMBER BOTTOM
D.

13 With a backsaw positioned just to the waste side of each line and held at about a 45° angle, define the sides of each pin by a saw kerf that connects the baseline on the back of the drawer front with the line drawn on the end grain indicating the forward limit of the tails.

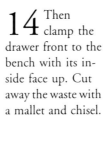

14 Then clamp the drawer front to the bench with its inside face up. Cut away the waste with a mallet and chisel.

15 Carefully (to avoid splitting the drawer front), shape the sides of the pins with the chisel.

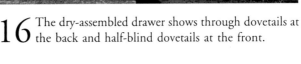

16 The dry-assembled drawer shows through dovetails at the back and half-blind dovetails at the front.

17 The procedure for dovetailing the sides of the case is the same as that used for the back of the drawer with two important differences: First, because of the board widths, there will be many more pins and tails, making joint fitting more time-consuming. Second, because the joint components are hardwood, they must be fit more carefully. Forcing a hardwood joint nearly always results in split stock.

18 Assemble the case around the bottom of the storage chamber. The edges of this bottom are housed in the groove on the inside faces of the four sides of the chest.

Clamping blocks permit the pressure to be exerted behind the pins. This allows the pins to protrude 1/16". After the glue has cured and the clamps have been removed, sand this excess away, making the ends of the pins flush with the sides of the case.

26

SHADOW BOX

White Oak

While sorting through my lumber in search of material for one of the projects in this book, I came across a single piece of white oak, less than four feet long, with a bit of curly figure on each side. It was too small for any of the pieces on my original list of projects, but I liked the curl and wanted to use it, so I designed this shadow box around the dimensions of that particular board.

When working with a limited amount of material as I was on this project, careful layout is essential. Before I attempted to dimension anything, I sketched out the various parts on the stock, frequently adjusting sizes and placements, searching for the best possible utilization of my material.

Once I arrived at that point, I cut out and thicknessed the various parts, smugly proud of the fact that I had used every bit of the curly figure. Unfortunately, as I was fitting one of the shelves, I miscut the length and there was no more curly-figure material from which a replacement part could be taken. The result is that, although all the parts for this piece were taken from the same board, one of the shelves has a bit less figure than the others.

MAKING THE SHADOW BOX

First, cut a ½″ × ⅜″ rabbet on the back inside edges of the two sides, into which the piece's back will later be fit. Cut through dovetails at each corner (see chapter twenty-five). After dry-fitting but before gluing the dovetails, cut the dadoes that will house the ends of the shelves on the inside faces of the two sides. When the shelves have been fit into the dadoes, glue and assemble the four sides of the case.

While the glue in the dovetail joints is curing, cut the dadoes in the two upper partitions and fit the partitions into them. Then glue and slide the partitions into place.

Below the half-circle at the top of the back, relieve the sides of the back so that they will fit into the rabbet cut into the back inside edges of the sides. Fasten the back in place with ¾″ no. 6 wood screws passing through the back, into the rabbet and into the back edges of the box's top and bottom. Then, sand and finish the shadow box.

MATERIALS LIST

A	Back	1 pc.	½ × 6⁵⁄₁₆ × 20⁹⁄₁₆
B	Side	2 pcs.	½ × 2 × 17⅜
C	Top and bottom	2 pcs.	½ × 1½ × 6⁵⁄₁₆
D	Shelf	3 pcs.	⅜ × 1½ × 5⁹⁄₁₆
E	Partition	2 pcs.	¼ × 1½ × 2⅛
F	Screws	10 pcs.	¾″ no. 6

**These are net measurements. Surplus should be added to dovetailed parts to allow them to be sanded flush.*

INTERPRETING HARDWOOD GRADES

The grading system used to indicate the quality of individual hardwood boards can be a little intimidating. In an effort to clarify that system, I spoke with the National Hardwood Lumber Association.

First, the system *is* complicated. The training course offered by the National Hardwood Lumber Association for people interested in a career in lumber grading consists of fourteen weeks of "intensive" training.

Second, although there are only nine commonly used grades, there are any number of specialized or combination grades used in the woodworking industry. However, the good news is that there are only four grades with which the average cabinetmaker need to be concerned. These are FAS, Selects, #1 Common, and #2A common.

Third, the grades are distinguished by the precentage of clear wood that could be taken from a board in cuttings not smaller than those specified on the chart below. For example, to be graded FAS, a board must be able to yield 83⅓ percent of its surface as clear wood when taken in cuttings not smaller than 4″ × 5′ or 3″ × 7′. (The odd percentages reflect the convention of measuring lumber in board feet, a unit consisting of the amount of material contained in a cutting 12″ × 12″ × 1′.)

Fourth, all grades, with the exception of Selects, are determined from the poor face of the board. This means that if a woodworker buys a board graded FAS, its good face is likely to offer a higher percentage of clear surface than is indicated on the chart.

	FAS	SELECT	#1 COM	#2A COM
Minimum Size Board	6″ × 8′	4″ × 6′	3″ × 4′	3″ × 4′
Minimum Size Cuttings	4″ × 5′ 3″ × 7′	4″ × 5′ 3″ × 7′	4″ × 2′ 3″ × 3″	3″ × 2′
Minimum Clear Yield	83⅓%	83⅓%	66⅔%	50%

**Please note that this chart is not intended to be a complete representation of any of the grades shown. It's intended only to offer some general guidelines.*

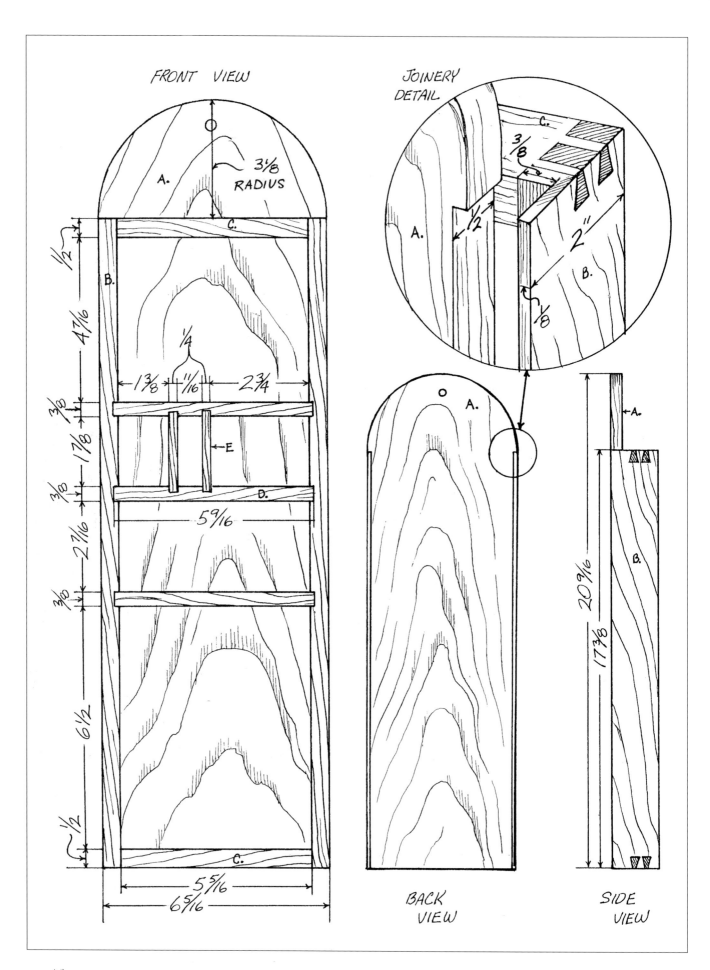

FRONT VIEW

JOINERY DETAIL

3⅛ RADIUS

A.

C.

B.

½

4⁷⁄₁₆

¼

1³⁄₈   ¹¹⁄₁₆   2¾

³⁄₈

1⅞

E

³⁄₈

2⁷⁄₁₆

5⁹⁄₁₆

D.

³⁄₈

6½

½

C.

5⁵⁄₁₆

6⁵⁄₁₆

C.

3⁄8

½

½

2"

B.

⅛

O   A.

BACK VIEW

A.

20⁹⁄₁₆

17⅜

B.

SIDE VIEW

27

DISPLAY CABINET

Cherry

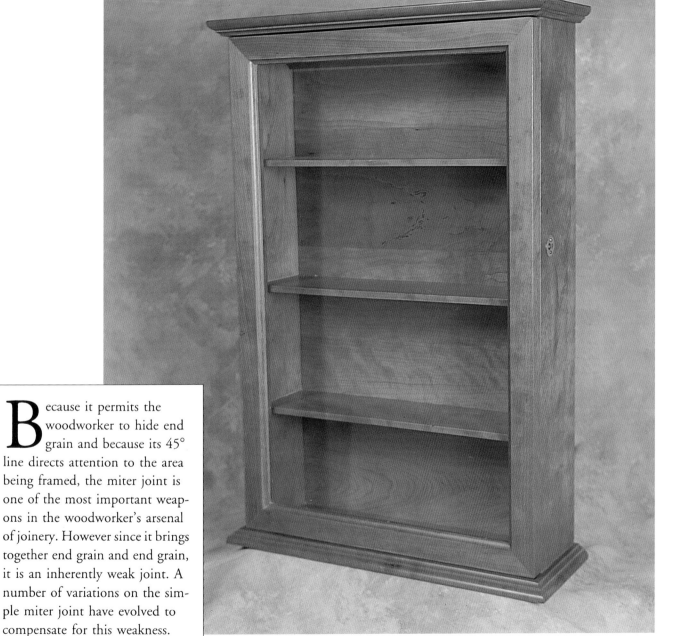

DESIGNED BY
JIM PIERCE

B ecause it permits the woodworker to hide end grain and because its 45° line directs attention to the area being framed, the miter joint is one of the most important weapons in the woodworker's arsenal of joinery. However since it brings together end grain and end grain, it is an inherently weak joint. A number of variations on the simple miter joint have evolved to compensate for this weakness. One variation, seen in the construction of the chess table elsewhere in this book, is the splined

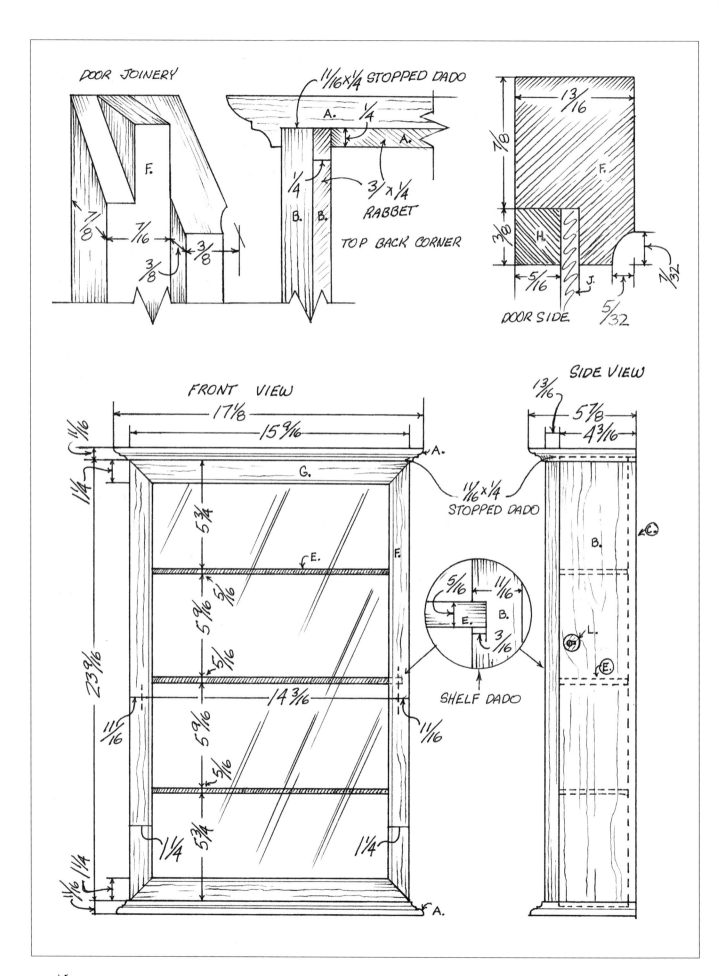

DOOR JOINERY

11/16 x 1/4 STOPPED DADO

A.   1/4

A.

3/ x 1/4
RABBET

TOP BACK CORNER

F.

7/8
7/16
3/8
3/8

1/4

B.   B.

13/16

7/8

F.

3/20

H.

5/16

5/32

J.

1/32

DOOR SIDE

FRONT VIEW

17 1/8

15 9/16

1/16

1/4

G.

A.

11/16 x 1/4
STOPPED DADO

SIDE VIEW

13/16

5 7/8

4 3/16

5 3/4

E.

5/16

F.

B.

C.

5 3/16

5/16

5/16

5/16
11/16

E.

B.

3/16

L.

G.

E.

23 9/16

14 3/16

11/16

11/16

SHELF DADO

5 9/16

5/16

1 1/4

5 3/4

1 1/4

1/16   1 1/4

A.

A.

miter. This spline not only increases the glue surface; it also allows face grain to be glued to face grain. The feathered miter, used in the construction of the Shaker-style mirror, is another variation of the basic miter joint, one offering the same advantages as the splined miter. The mitered bridle joint used in the construction of the door on this cherry display cabinet is still another variation, one including tenons on the door's sides which fit into mortises cut into the miters on the door's top and bottom. This joint offers the strength of tenons which are an actual part of the door's sides. It does, however, provide less glue surface than either the splined or feathered miter joints.

MAKING THE DISPLAY CABINET

After milling the stock to the required thicknesses, lengths, and widths, form the moulded edge on the front and ends of the cabinet top and bottom. Then, cut $^{11}/_{16}$″ × $^{1}/_4$″ stopped dadoes on the top surface of the bottom and the bottom surface of the top (see chapter five). These dadoes will house the ends of the cabinet sides. Cut a $^{3}/_8$″ × $^{1}/_4$″ rabbet across the back of the cabinet top and bottom connecting the dadoes. Cut the same rabbet on the back, inside edges of the cabinet sides. These four rabbets will house the perimeter of the cabinet back. Finally, cut three $^{3}/_{16}$″ × $^{5}/_{16}$″ dadoes across the inside surface of the cabinet sides to house the ends of the shelves.

Then assemble the case with glue and screws passing down through the top into the sides, and up through the bottom into the sides. Screw the back to the cabinet sides, top, bottom and the backs of the shelves. These screws

pass through oversized holes to allow the back to expand and contract in response to seasonal changes in humidity.

Begin door construction by running the moulded edge on the front inside corner of the frame stock. Cut a $^{3}/_8$″ × $^{7}/_{16}$″ rabbet on the back inside edge. Then cut the mitered bridle joint. You can do this with a backsaw and a chisel or with a stack of dado cutters on the table saw, holding the work in a Universal Jig.

The glass is held in its rabbet with the four tack strips.

MATERIALS LIST			
A	Top and bottom	2 pcs.	$^{11}/_{16}$ × $5^{7}/_8$ × $17^{1}/_8$
B	Side	2 pcs.	$^{11}/_{16}$ × $4^{3}/_{16}$ × $24^{1}/_{16}$
C	Back	1 pc.	$^{3}/_8$ × $14^{13}/_{16}$ × $24^{1}/_{16}$
D	Cleat	1 pc.	$^{13}/_{16}$ × $1^{1}/_4$ × $14^{3}/_{16}$
E	Shelf	3 pcs.	$^{5}/_{16}$ × $3^{3}/_{16}$ × $14^{9}/_{16}$
Door			
F	Door side	2 pcs.	$^{13}/_{16}$ × $1^{1}/_4$ × $23^{9}/_{16}$
G	Door top and bottom	2 pcs.	$^{13}/_{16}$ × $1^{1}/_4$ × $15^{9}/_{16}$
H	Vertical tack strip	2 pcs.	$^{1}/_4$ × $^{3}/_8$ × $21^{3}/_4$
I	Horizontal tack strip	2 pcs.	$^{1}/_4$ × $^{3}/_8$ × $12^{15}/_{16}$
J	Glass	1 pc.	$^{1}/_8$ × $13^{3}/_4$ × $21^{3}/_4$
Hardware			
K	Hinge	2 pcs.	1 × $1^{3}/_4$
L	Lock	1 pc.	$1^{5}/_8$ × $1^{7}/_8$
M	Screws	various	

These are net measurements. Surplus should be added to door sides to permit joints to be sanded flush.

28

SIX-WOOD BOX

Mixed Woods

Sometimes the simplest ideas are the best. One day, as I worked on the pieces for this book, I stopped for a moment and stood—ankle-deep in sawdust, shavings and scrap—looking around my crowded shop. I had an idea. What if I took the rips of cherry, walnut, ash, and maple leaning against the shop wall and what if I threw in some sassafras and white oak and what if I arranged them so that they looked good and what if I then glued them and planed them flat? Could I use that panel as a top and bottom for a small jewelry-type box?

Maybe. But it seemed too easy, and that afternoon as I ripped and jointed the scrap to a consistent thickness, as I slathered on the glue, and as I brought the strips together in the clamps, I had the feeling that I was wasting my time. It couldn't possibly work. It was too easy.

But now, several months later, the piece sits on the dresser in our bedroom, and every time I pass I find myself running my fingers across its multi-colored top.

INSTALLING HARDWARE

Many years ago, I made a drop-leaf walnut wall desk with a number of variously sized pigeonholes. I remember the satisfaction I felt fitting each of the little dividers into its dadoes. I remember the pains I took to smooth the wood with a variety of sandpaper grits. I also remember visiting the hardware store in search of a lid support that would hold the drop leaf at the proper angle so that it could be used as a writing surface.

I found the brass support that I had envisioned for my desk and I took it home and tried to install it. I tried it one way and then another and another, each time making screw holes in my carefully sanded walnut, until I realized, with a growing sense of panic, that it simply wasn't going to work, that the arrangement of pigeonholes I'd designed left no room for the operation of this lid support.

I searched the mail order catalogs next (at that time, there weren't nearly as many to choose from). But nothing I found there looked any more likely to work in the tight confines of my desk than what I'd already tried.

Rule number one for makers of furniture and wooden-ware: *Buy the hardware first.* Buy it before construction starts, before a single stick of wood is cut, before even the finishing touches are put on the design. Buy the hardware first because what the project requires may not be available or, if available, may not work as envisioned.

What happened to the wall desk? I did finish it, and we did use it in our home for several years. We, then, later gave it to a friend. Although I haven't seen it for ten or eleven years and have attempted to blot its memory from my mind, I believe that my solution to the problem of the drop leaf support involved a length of noisy and inelegant brass chain.

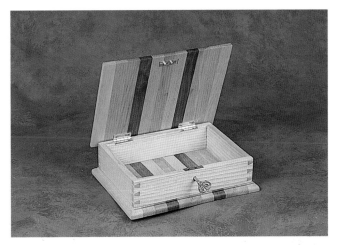

The opened six-wood box shows the lock installed in the front.

Before beginning work on this small box, I waited for my hardware to arrive.

Begin construction with the glued-up panel from which the top and bottom are cut. Shuffle around a number of rips approximately 1″ wide until a pleasing arrangement is found. Then glue-up and clamp these rips. After the glue is cured, you can plane the panel (see chapter five) cut out the box's top and bottom, and mould them on a shaper or a table-mounted router.

Dimension and dovetail sidewall material together (see chapter twenty-five). Fasten the bottom in place with a number of screws passing through oversized holes that allow expansion and contraction of the bottom in response to seasonal changes in humidity.

1 Install the hinges on the back wall of the box. This process begins with careful layout. Lines marking the ends of the hinge leaves are squared across the back wall of the box. Then, additional lines marking the depth of the hinge mortises are drawn. Set these lines so that the top surfaces of the top leaves are flush with the top edge of the box's back wall.

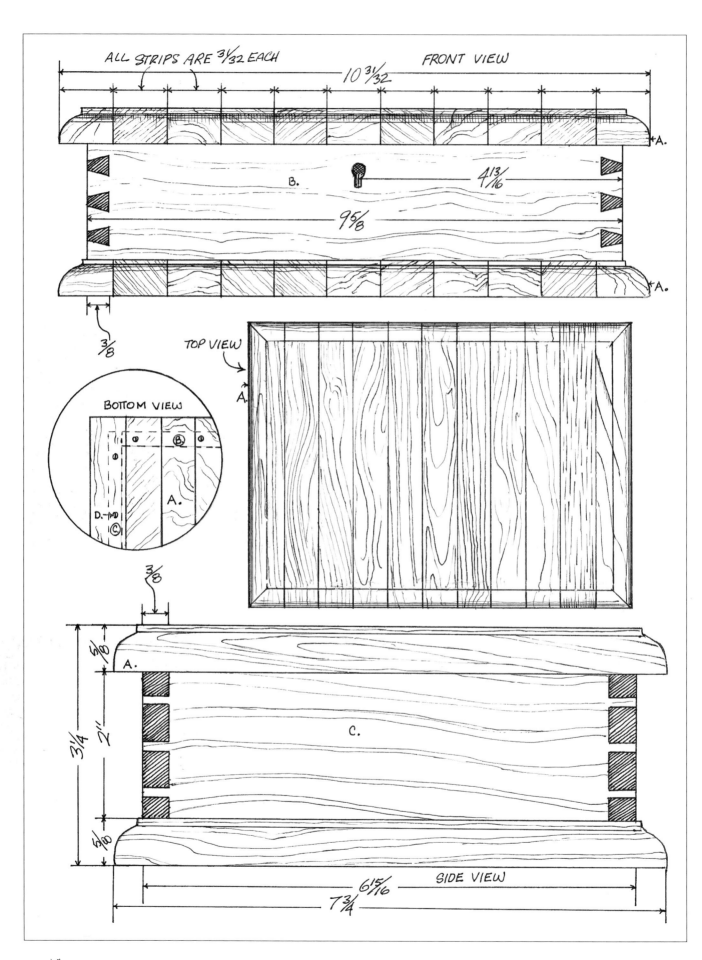

ALL STRIPS ARE ³¹/₃₂ EACH   FRONT VIEW

10 ³¹/₃₂

A.

B.   4¹³/₁₆

9⁵/₈

A.

³/₈

TOP VIEW

A.

BOTTOM VIEW

D. C

A.

³/₈

⁵/₈

A.

³/₄   2"   C.

⁵/₈

6¹⁵/₁₆

7³/₄

SIDE VIEW

2 A series of shallow chisel cuts lifts wood from the mortises. This will be removed by working the chisel back, from the opposite direction.

MATERIALS LIST

A	Top and bottom	2 pcs.	$5/8 \times 7\frac{3}{4} \times 10^{31}/_{32}$
B	Front and back	2 pcs.	$3/8 \times 2 \times 9\frac{5}{8}$
C	Side	2 pcs.	$3/8 \times 2 \times 6^{15}/_{16}$
D	Screws	12 pcs.	$1\frac{1}{4}$ no. 8
E	Hinge	2 pcs.	$1\frac{1}{2} \times 7/8$
F	Box lock	1 pc.	$1\frac{1}{2} \times 1$

*Front, back and side length measurements are net. Surplus should be added so that dovetail can be sanded flush.
*Hinges and lock were ordered from Constantine's Hardware.
*Reading from left to right, the woods in the top are as follows: hard maple, white oak, cherry, walnut, sassafras, cherry, sassafras, walnut, cherry, white oak, hard maple. The box's walls are made of ash.

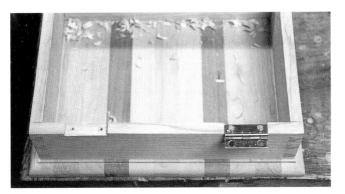

3 After cutting the mortises, install the hinges. Take care to accurately align the hinges so that both hinge pins open on the same axis.

5 Remove hinges from the back wall so they can be installed on the lid. Here, a scratch awl is being used to punch a starting hole for the drill bit in the center of the circle marking the screw holes in the hinges.

4 When the hinges have been fastened to the box's back wall, invert the box over the lid and tape in place. Then mark hinge locations very carefully.

6 After installing the hinges on the lid, fasten the hinges' other leaves into the mortises previously cut into the box's back wall.

7 Next, install the brass box lock. Again, careful layout is essential. Square a centerline across the top edge of the box's front wall and draw the mortise for the lock on the top edge and inside face.

Then extend the centerline down the front face of the box's front wall, and lay out the keyhole along this line. Drill a ¼" hole above a ⅛" hole to remove most of the waste necessary for the creation of the keyhole.

8 Four ³⁄₁₆" holes remove much of the waste for the mortise that will house the main body of the lock.

9 The completed mortise can be seen from the back.

10 After installing the lock in the box's front wall, locate the strike plate on the bottom side of the lid. The first step in that process is locking that strike plate in place with the key.

Here, the strike plate can be seen locked facedown. Notice the two bumps on the back side of the strike plate. When the lid is closed and tapped firmly, these two bumps leave depressions on the lid's bottom surface, locating the strike plate on the lid.

11 In this photo, the two depressions can be seen near the upper edge of the lid. After the lid has been clamped face-down on the benchtop, position the strike plate so that the two bumps on its upper side are located in these depressions. Then draw a line around the strike plate and the mortise cut.

12 Cut the mortise in which the strike plate will sit. The lock is now fully functional.

BENTWOOD BOX WITH SNAP-FIT LID

Walnut, Hard Maple

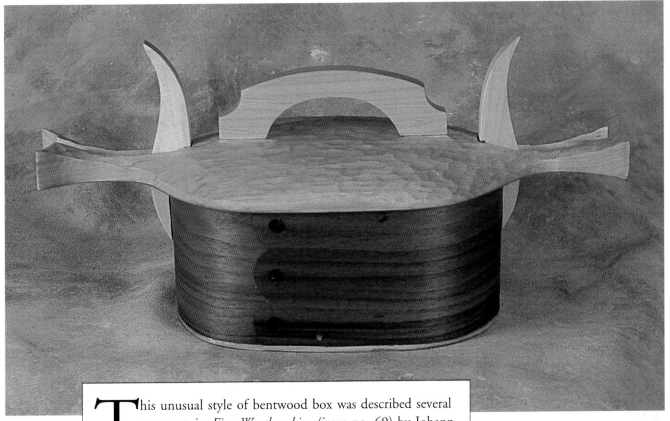

This unusual style of bentwood box was described several years ago in *Fine Woodworking* (issue no. 69) by Johann Hopstad. According to Hopstad, bentwood boxes have a long and varied history in Europe, having been used there for everything from luggage to lunch boxes.

What is striking about this particular style is the snap-fit lid. Tension in the bentwood sidewalls holds the two upright clasps in a position that locks them against the lid. To open the box, the clasps must be spread with the thumbs (as shown in the photos on page 124). To close the box, the lid is pressed into place until the catches on the clasps snap into their locking positions.

MAKING THE BENTWOOD BOX

Work begins with the construction of a bending form for the main body of the box. Mine consists of a stack of spruce 2 × 4's laminated together and band-sawn and sanded to the box's inside profile. On the side of the form that will shape the front of the box, the face of the form is undercut for the lap of material beneath the box's glue joint. A thin strip of metal (in my case, aluminum siding) is screwed to the form creating an opening into which the end of the sidewall material can be slipped as that material is wrapped around the form.

The next step is acquiring material for the sidewalls of the box (see chapter two for a detailed discussion).

After the sidewall material has been soaked (for twenty-four hours in cool water, followed by ten minutes in warm water), wrapped around the form, and clamped in place, it should dry for four or five days. At that time, remove it from the form and cut the lap joint. For this particular example, I drilled three holes in the joint, sandwiching in three bits of peacock feather between the lapping laminations so that the feather was visible through the holes. The joint is then glued and clamped using the bending form and the caul both to protect the material from the clamps and to preserve the box's oval shape while the glue cures. (this process is described in some detail in chapter two).

Cut out the clasps and the handle next. Thicknesses can vary, but the thickness of the clasps must be accurately transferred to the stock that will later become the lid so that the walls of the notches fit snugly against the clasps.

When you have selected the lid material, place the box's bentwood sidewalls on that material and draw a line around its circumference. Next, establish a centerline running from one end of the box to the other. This centerline is necessary in order to lay out the notches that will house the clasps.

Next, sketch the outside profile of the lid. There is considerable freedom in establishing this profile since the notch placements are the only critical locations on the lid. Then cut the lid's outside profile on the band saw.

Once the lid has been shaped, the handle is affixed. I taped the handle in place, turned the lid over, and drove a couple of wood screws up through the lid and into the handle.

Make the bottom next. After thicknessing the stock to $\frac{7}{16}$", place the box's bentwood sidewalls on the bottom material. Profile the inside and outside of the sidewalls. On the band saw, cut the bottom profile, keeping the saw kerf approximately $\frac{1}{16}$" outside the pencil line that marked the outside circumference of the sidewalls. Then, clamping the bottom in a vise, cut away the extra $\frac{1}{16}$" of material with a block plane, to remove the saw marks.

Mark the rabbet around the bottom circumference with a line $\frac{5}{16}$" from the top surface of the bottom. Next, with a dovetail saw, make a shallow cut along that line. This saw kerf represents the bottom of the rabbet. With a chisel, cut the rabbet to the depth marked by the line traced around the inside face of the sidewalls. Once the bottom has been fit, sand the parts and assemble the box using $\frac{1}{8}$" wooden pegs to both fasten the walls to the bottom and the clasps to the walls.

MATERIALS LIST			
A	Top	1 pc.	$1 \times 7\frac{1}{4} \times 15\frac{1}{2}$
B	Sidewall	1 pc.	$\frac{1}{16} \times 3\frac{1}{2} \times 30$
C	Bottom	1 pc.	$\frac{7}{16} \times 6\frac{1}{4} \times 8\frac{1}{2}$
D	Clasps	2 pcs.	$\frac{1}{2} \times 1\frac{1}{8} \times 7\frac{1}{4}$
E	Handle	1 pc.	$\frac{9}{16} \times 1\frac{3}{4} \times 6\frac{1}{8}$

Measurements for lid, bottom and clasps must be taken from the dimensions of the sidewall, which are, in turn, determined by the size of the bending form.

OPENING THE BOX

1 Place your thumbs on the tops of the box's clasps while your fingers grasp the fishtail ends of the lid. Spread open the clasps and lift the lid. To close, press the lid down against the clasps until it snaps into place.

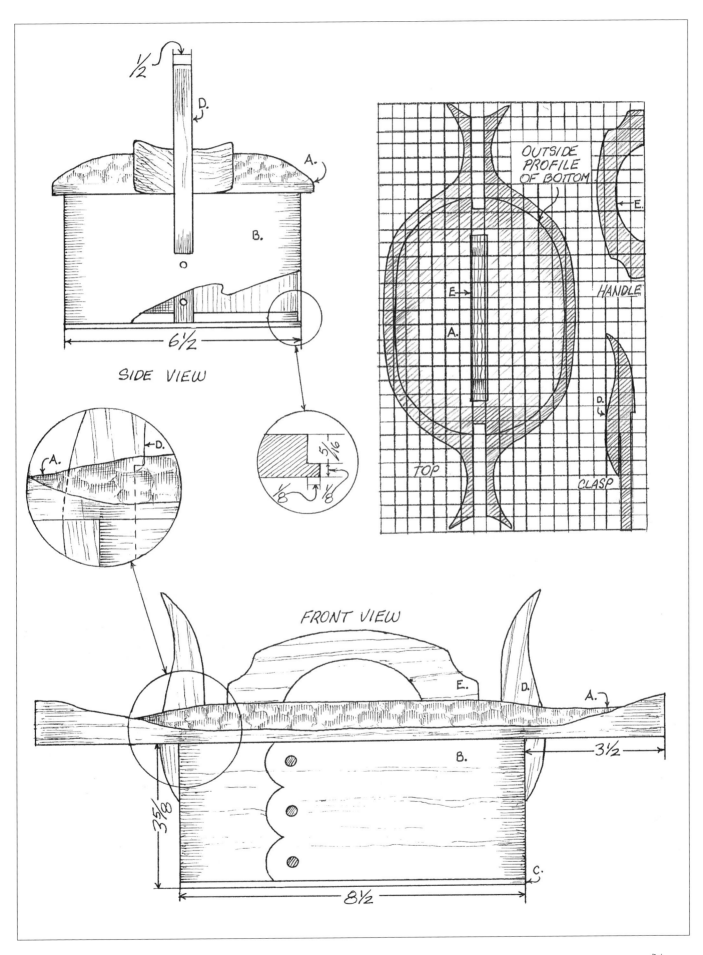

½

D.

A.

B.

o

6½

SIDE VIEW

A.

D.

5/16

⅛   ⅛

OUTSIDE
PROFILE
OF BOTTOM

E.

HANDLE

E.

A.

D.

TOP

CLASP

FRONT VIEW

E.

D.

A.

B.

3½

35/100

C.

8½

This close up of the box side reveals peacock feather inlay in the holes, a very unique design element.

BENDING FORM

1 A block at the base of the bending form allows a vise to hold it. After wrapping the soaked, resawn stock around the form, clamp the caul to the form to hold it in place. Cut an opening in the top of the form for the clamp head.

MAKING THE LID

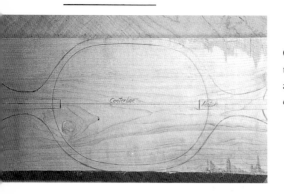

1 The layout of the lid is shown. Careful planning at this stage will ensure a lid that snaps cleanly into place.

2 If the surface of the lid is to be shaped, flat surfaces must be left for the base of the handle.

MAKING THE BOTTOM

1 Define the bottom of the rabbet that will receive the sidewalls by a shallow saw cut made all around the bottom.

2 Cut the rabbet with a chisel. Here, the chisel is cutting across end grain. After cutting another ¾″ of the rabbet, reverse the bottom in the vise in order to cut back to that point from the other side.

3 The various parts have been cut and fit and are ready for assembly. Notice the widened section of the rabbet which will receive the lapped section of the sidewalls. Notice, too, the notches for the bottoms of the clasps.

PEGS

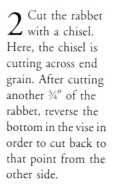

1 This shows the ends of two pegs driven through the sidewall into the clasp. Below, to the left, is one of the pegs holding the bottom and sidewall together. Drill a hole before inserting these pegs.

INDEX